Ephesians
Sealed in Christ

Kristi W. Cook

WESTBOW
PRESS®

A DIVISION OF THOMAS NELSON
& ZONDERVAN

WestBow Press books may be ordered through booksellers or by contacting:

WestBow Press
A Division of Thomas Nelson & Zondervan
1663 Liberty Drive
Bloomington, IN 47403
www.westbowpress.com
1 (866) 928-1240

ISBN: 978-1-9736-1424-1 (sc)
ISBN: 978-1-9736-1423-4 (e)

Library of Congress Control Number: 2018900536

Print information available on the last page.

WestBow Press rev. date: 01/26/2018

Contents

Preface

I am completely humbled that you are reading this. During the journey through Ephesians that I had with the Lord, I fell in love with intentional Bible study. I pray you do the same. As you read and work through this study, read the passages and pray over them each day that the Lord would speak to you before you read how He spoke to me.

This study covers every single passage in Ephesians. After you complete this study, you will not only know every detail of Ephesians, but you will also know Him better. I hope the desire to study His Word will grow in you so strongly that you cannot put His Word down.

I could not have done this without the encouragement from my Bible study ladies at First Baptist Church of Pascagoula. Your dedication and eagerness to learn, your faithfulness, and your encouragement always inspired me to press on even when I didn't think I could.

I also could not have done this without my Ephesians prayer team. Angela, Carol, Caroline, and Cyndi, your prayers were an irreplaceable gift. There are truly no words that can adequately express my gratefulness for you. To know you all intentionally covered me in prayer is indescribable. *Thank you!*

And to my family, especially my children, Jameson and Amelia Rose, who watched as our dining room table was covered in Ephesians for years and who patiently waited for me while I studied and wrote. Your dedication in service to the Lord at a young age inspired me every day to follow His will. I *love* you, and thank you.

To my husband, Jay, who answered every question when I did not understand, typed hundreds of pages for our study, and fact-checked the content, you amaze me. Your service and love for the Lord is what inspires us all. Thank you for encouraging me to continue when I thought I was done (many times). *I love you.*

And to my parents for raising me to love Him, I am forever grateful. Mom, you were the one that taught me to seek Him first every morning. Dad, you encourage me in everything I do. I love you both so much.

I'm just a girl still figuring things out, but I'm loving the Lord more through it all and through each new day of studying His Word. Please visit my blog: www. kristiwcook.com

Day 1

Background of Paul and Ephesus

Acts 18:19–21; 19

As we begin our journey into the letter of Ephesians, let's get a little background knowledge of the relationship between Paul and the cosmopolitan city of Ephesus, which was so dear to his heart and ministry. We are going to hunker down in Acts today. The letter of Acts is beautifully written by Luke, giving accounts of the Christian message across vast areas. "But; you will receive power when the Holy Spirit comes on you, and you will be my witnesses in Jerusalem, and in all Judea and Samaria, and to the ends of the earth" (Acts 1:8–9).

These were the words spoken by Jesus to His apostles when they questioned Him about restoring the kingdom of Israel. Jesus made it very clear that the kingdom of God and the message are for everyone.

Fast-forward to the missionary ministry of Paul and Barnabas. This will be a lightening-quick, condensed version of Acts today! We have to cover this in a day so that we can get to Ephesians! Paul and Barnabas were sent to Paphos, Perga, Antioch in Pisidia, Iconium, Derbe, Attaliea, and Antioch.

On a side note, I would love to tell you that I learned about this missionary voyage while studying a map of the Mediterranean Sea or something. Quite the contrary! While teaching a fourth-grade Sunday school class, I took my students on a pretend voyage around the room while teaching them about Paul and Barnabas and their missionary lives. You see, my friends, God uses every moment you serve to prepare you for another opportunity to serve. While voyaging around that classroom and stopping at sites made out of construction paper, I didn't know I would be opening up a Bible study with that same route, but God did!

The reason I wanted to highlight their missionary journey together might not be what you thought. Paul and Barnabas preached the good news all over together. Together, they strengthened disciples and encouraged them in their faith. They prayed and fasted together. They appointed elders and together helped to organize churches. They endured and suffered many hardships together. Then a disagreement tore them apart.

Read Acts 15:36–41.

What was the disagreement?

_____

_____

This is a tough one. On the one hand, you hate to see a ministry team fall apart over a disagreement. On the other hand, you see in scripture that Paul, Barnabas, and Mark went on to do incredible things for God. God knew even greater things could be done if they parted ways.

If anything, what we can learn is that God can use anything for His glory if allowed. *Sometimes our biggest distractions can become His greatest achievements*—that is, if we give them to Him! Barnabas was an encourager. Paul was an organized rule follower. Both men had powerful ministries.

Fast-forward again!

Read Acts 18:1–3 and 9–11.

Who did Paul meet?

_____

_____

We see a new friendship forming between this couple and Paul, one that will lead to a ministry together. They shared a common trade. What was it?

How long did he stay with them?

_____

_____

God can use godly friendships to strengthen your walk and His kingdom. Do you have those kinds of friends? I encourage you to find one—not just someone to shop with, have coffee with, and set up play dates with but someone you study the Word with, someone who encourages you, someone who prays with you, and someone you pray for. It will be life-changing!

Read Acts 18:19–21.

They arrived in Ephesus. And so have we on our journey! And just as quickly as Paul arrived in verse 19, they set sail from Ephesus in verse 21.

Hold on. We are almost done with this background day. And don't sigh. But I need you to read all of Acts 19! Because just as Paul promised to return to Ephesus, he did. And he stayed for three years. A spoonful of sugar helps the medicine go down! You need all this background information to truly understand the meaning of Paul's letter to the Ephesians.

Read Acts 19.

- Go back to verse 2. This verse hit my heart like a ton of bricks! So many have still not heard even today.

- What stands out to you in verse 10?

_____

- In verse 19, it is briefly mentioned that the burned scrolls were valued at fifty thousand drachmas. Why was this important?

_____

- Is there anything in our lives that we need to remove?

_____

- What started the riot in Ephesus?

_____

- During the riot in Ephesus, what do you think about regarding what the disciples did in verse 30?

_____

- How could so many put their hope and faith in Artemis?

_____

- Do we ever put our hope and faith in something other than Jesus?

_____

¹Can you imagine the boldness it took for Paul to preach the Word of God to a town that was solely devoted to the worship of Artemis (Diana)?

Think back to the vision he had in Acts 18:9–10. What did God tell Paul to do in this vision?

Here you have the scene set for the capital of the Roman province of Asia—the city of Ephesus. It is home of the temple of Artemis, one of the seven wonders of the ancient world, and it has a population of about 350,000. Demetrius, a silversmith, started the riot in Ephesus, pointing out that the worship of Artemis (Diana) was their only source of income. Demetrius was just one of many who made a living by making silver shrines of Artemis (Acts 19:24). And through the power of Jesus Christ, one man (Paul) chose obedience, and he changed an entire city in the process.

We are about to read what has become one of my favorite passages in scripture. (Don't hold me to that because I will mention other favorites later!) First, let's start with verse 1 of chapter 20, and then we will move to my favorite! "When the uproar had ended, Paul sent for the disciples and, after encouraging them, said good-bye and set out for Macedonia" (Acts 20:1).

Next, you are going to read the only recorded sermon from Paul to Christians and the only sermon recorded from his third missionary journey. Keep in mind he is leaving people he has loved and ministered to for several years. This passage has become one of my favorites for bittersweet reasons. As a pastor's wife, I know how hard it is to leave a church that you have loved and has loved you back. But Paul knew it was time to go. God was calling him to move on. When God calls, you go.

Read Paul's farewell to the Ephesian elders in Acts 20:16–38.

What does Paul warn them to be "on guard" for in verses 30–31? _____

_____

When he was finished with the sermon, what did he do in verse 36? _____

_____

Can you imagine the scene? The passionate prayers being lifted up? The tears? The embracing of godly men who had served together?

Sisters, please kneel where you are (with fellow Bible study ladies if you can) and pray for your church. The enemy is lurking to destroy anything that is for the kingdom of God. Look at the obstacles and distractions Paul faced in just the passages that we studied today. Get ready for Ephesians. The battle awaits you. It's where you will find your spiritual armor!

Day 2

Spiritual Blessings in Christ

Ephesians 1:1–14

As we begin our journey today into the first chapter of Ephesians, my heart is heavy but full of joy. I want you to know that I am not a Bible scholar. I did not go to seminary … yet! I have not had a mentor who has guided me through the Word. I've not only wanted that mentor and degree, but I've also prayed for them. However, a few years ago, I sat down with my Bible and some commentaries and prayed that God would reveal a fresh Word, and He did! I wish you could see my dining room table now. It is covered with Bibles, commentaries, scrap pieces of paper, dictionaries, and sticky notes! I still long for that degree and mentor, but now I don't have to wait for those to guide me in the Word. God can do that Himself!

Read John 14:26.

Who will teach us? _____

Pray that the Holy Spirit will guide and direct you as you study the entire book of Ephesians.

Ready? Let's dive in heart first!

Read Ephesians 1:1–14.

Fill in the blanks from verse 3. "Praise be to the God and Father of our Lord Jesus Christ, who has blessed us in the heavenly realms with every _____ _____ ____ _____."

Paul wrote the letter to the Ephesians from a prison cell in Rome. He opens his letter to the faithful saints in Ephesus (church members he served with) by reminding them of our spiritual blessings. There are seven in all (a number that is used often in scripture) listed throughout Ephesians 1:4–14. Please take note that these spiritual blessings are heavenly, not earthly.

Spiritual Blessings in Christ

1. Election

"For he chose us in him before the creation of the world to be holy and blameless in his sight" (Ephesians 1:4).

Please read 2 Peter 1:10–11.

Merriam-Webster defines *election* as "predestination to eternal life," with synonyms such as *choice* and *selection*.[2] Let's go a little further. We can see that *Merriam-Webster* defines *predestination* as follows: "the doctrine that God in consequence of his foreknowledge of all events infallibly guides those who are destined for salvation."[3]

Oh, sister! He has elected you and chosen you, wanting to guide you to salvation! If you have never accepted that nomination into eternity, I urge you to do so now. Pray this prayer: "Lord, You chose me and knew me before I even entered the world. Be the Lord over my life and my heart. Guide me to do Your will. I am Yours."

Please know that there is not a magical prayer that gives you salvation. It's a decision that you must follow through with. You allow God to be Lord over your life.

Please speak to someone if you prayed that for the first time—a pastor, Bible study leader, Christian friend, etc.

2. Adoption

"He predestined us to be adopted as his sons through Jesus Christ, in accordance with his pleasure and will" (Ephesians 1:5).

Please read Romans 8:14–15.

"Spirit of sonship" means adoption.

Merriam-Webster defines *adopt* as follows: "(1) to take by choice into a relationship (2) to accept formally and put into effect," with synonyms such as *accept*, *take*, and *embrace*.[4]

How does it make you feel to know you were taken by choice into a relationship, embraced, accepted, and adopted by God?

_____

_____

Look back at the second definition of *adopt*. If God formally accepts us, how can we further explain the "put into effect" part?

_____

_____

You can dangerously wrap up your entire self-worth on feeling accepted. You can kill your spirit here on earth trying. We long for acceptance and may temporarily find it. The only acceptance we will ever need is the adoption through Christ. Praise God!

The next two go hand-in-hand.

3. Redemption

"But now, this is what the LORD says—he who created you, Jacob, he who formed you, Israel: 'Do not fear, for I have redeemed you; I have summoned you by name; you are mine'" (Isaiah 43:1).

We have redemption through His blood. In Old Testament law, a sacrifice had to be made. Blood had to be shed as an atonement, a temporary removal or cleansing of sins. Jesus became that sacrifice for us.

4. Forgiveness of Sin

"In him we have redemption through his blood, the forgiveness of sins, in accordance with the riches of God's grace that he lavished on us with all wisdom and understanding" (Ephesians 1:7–8)

Read Colossians 1:13–14.

You know that brick wall you feel between you and God sometimes? Or when your prayers seem to bounce back from the ceiling? That is unconfessed sin, my friend, and it applies to even the ones you think are small. Each one adds a brick to the already existing wall.

He paid our ransom and rescued us through redemption. He offers us a pardon and mercy through the forgiveness of our sins.

What are you waiting for? Go knock that brick wall down! Stop now and ask God to show you any unconfessed sin that serves as a barrier between you and Him.

Read Psalm 139:23–24.

5. Mystery of His Will

"And he made known to us the mystery of his will according to his good pleasure which he purposed in Christ" (Ephesians 1:9).

Read Romans 16:25–26.

Read Colossians 1:26–27.

Read 1 Timothy 3:16.

What is the mystery? _____

I love a good mystery! I also love to look back in scripture and see how God moved in so many mighty ways leading up to Jesus.

Merriam-Webster defines *mystery* as a religious truth that one can know only by revelation and cannot fully understand. I found the origin of the word *mystery* fascinating. In Medieval Latin, it was *misterium*, and it was derived from the word *minister.*[5]

Do you see these puzzle pieces fitting together? Our mystery (minister) is Jesus Christ!

6. Sealed with the Holy Spirit

I could squeal with joy over this one! A *seal* is an impression, something that secures, a closure.

"And you also were included in Christ when you heard the word of truth, the gospel of your salvation. Having believed, you were marked in him with a seal" (Ephesians 1:13).

Please read John 6:27 and 2 Corinthians 1:21–22.

It was a bittersweet day when my family had to clean out my grandparents' house after they had passed away. The sadness of the day was overcome a little by the excitement of the treasures we hoped to find in the attic. To our dismay, the only sure thing we found was the right to declare my grandparents Southern pack rats. There were empty jars by the hundreds, all of which missed the opportunity to be filled with my grandfather's famous nuts and bolts (a treasured family snack mix recipe that was given out only to his best of friends, family, and any acquaintance). There were boxes of ceiling tiles and even boxes of old napkins and paper from the local paper mill where he worked! None of this stuff was even garage sale material, much less treasure! Deciding to call it a day, we pulled down a dusty old trunk and closed up the attic. But when I opened the lid of that trunk, I found our treasure. My grandfather's army trunk was filled with pictures, artwork, fabrics, and souvenirs from the countries he had visited while serving his own. Tucked away at the bottom were dozens of letters he had written to my grandmother. He was serving his country while missing his bride, penning his fears, joy, and love. Every single letter had SWAK handwritten on the outside of the envelope (sealed with a kiss). My grandfather sealed his letters with a kiss making an impression on my grandmother that she was his love.

Those letters are an inspiration to me and a look into my grandparents' young love and life. They are truly a gift. My grandfather's SWAK was heartwarming and sweet. We, however, are offered a much stronger seal.

Do you feel the love and protection of God's seal on your life? Why, or why not?

_____

_____

Dr. Joe McKeever had this to say about this particular verse in Ephesians:

Child of God, when the Lord saved you, he sealed you in. That's why you cannot fall out of salvation. He didn't use childproof packaging but the stronger stuff: foolproof and devil-proof packaging. You are locked in, belted in, strapped in, shut up, guarded, sealed and secure. Thank you, precious Father, for a salvation that does not depend on my works, my feelings, my friends or my fears!

7. Our Inheritance

"Who is a deposit guaranteeing our inheritance until the redemption of those who are God's possession – to the praise of his glory" (Ephesians 1:14).
Read Hebrews 9:15 and 1 Peter 1:4.
What do these verses mean to you?_____

_____

When you deposit money at the bank, it's usually in an account that can draw interest. Your money is secure and will remain so, but it's gaining more.

If you are a child of God, sealed and deposited with the Holy Spirit, your spot in heaven secure. Is that enough for you? Are you making deposits into the kingdom of God?

_____

We would all love to leave our children with an inheritance that would keep them secure, but what kind of kingdom legacy are we leaving them?

_____

_____

Well, there you have it! All seven spiritual blessings! Whew! And this is just the first fourteen verses!

Which spiritual blessing spoke the most to you today, and why?

_____

_____

If this was your first time reading about spiritual blessings, praise God! If you already had some knowledge of these truths, praise God as well! And just as Paul used the opening of his letter to the faithful ones in Ephesus to remind them of these spiritual blessings, we, the faithful ones of today, should be reminded as well. Take a moment to thank God for each and every one of those spiritual blessings.

Day 3

Thanksgiving

Ephesians 1:15–16

I hope you are ready to flip some pages in your Bible! We are going all over the New Testament today. Hop on board and fasten your seat belts. *This is a ride that could change your life.* That makes me think of that Colossal Coaster VBS song, and now it is stuck in my head! Yes, God can put a VBS song in your head and use it to guide you to something bigger. Hold on! Here we go!

I *love* and *despise* roller coasters. I'm usually talked into riding them on family vacations by my husband, children, and nieces. They all love my reactions—my obnoxious screams, the buildup of anxiety as I wait in line, and the pictures that are almost as fun to them as the ride itself. I know one thing for sure. I would never ride them alone. I'm so thankful for these family trips. We make the best memories together. I'm so thankful I never have to ride alone!

The following information is about roller coasters. Go there with God. Allow Him to speak to you through *anything*!

"Wooden versus Steel"

Wooden roller coasters provide a very different ride and experience from steel roller coasters. While they are traditionally (less capable) than a steel coaster when it comes to inversions and elements, wooden coasters instead rely on an often (rougher) and more "wild" ride, as well as a more psychological approach to inducing (fear.) Their structures and track, which usually move anywhere from a few inches to a few feet with a passing train, give a (sense of unreliability) and the "threat" of collapse or disregard for safety. Of course, this assumption is purely mental, and wooden roller coaster supports and track systems are designed to (sway with the force.) If the track and structure are too rigid, they will (break under the strain) of the passing train. The swaying of the track reduces the force applied per second like a (shock absorber).[6]

- Do you feel "less capable" at times?
- Do you feel like your life is "often rougher" than others?
- Are you consumed with "fear?"
- Is your life surrounded by people who "give a sense of unreliability?"
- Do you feel like when things are going smoothly, you all of a sudden have to "sway with the force" that daily life can bring?
- Do you sometimes feel like you "will break under the strain?"

Do you feel like that comparison of roller coasters just summed up your life? Please explain.

_____

_____

Just like a wooden roller coaster needs a shock absorber, so do we, my friend, and His name is Jesus. Paul knew all too well the ups and downs as well as the twists and turns that life had to offer. And that is precisely why he had an attitude of gratitude for fellow believers. Our focus passage today is Ephesians 1:15–16. Please read and record the two verses here.

_____

_____

Paul wrote thirteen books in the New Testament, all of them letters—Romans through Philemon.

Please read the following verses from many of Paul's letters. Notice the reoccurring theme. Make any notes you feel are necessary.

Romans 1:8–10: _____

_____

1 Corinthians 1:4–6: _____

_____

Philippians 1:3–6: _____

_____

Colossians 1:3–4: _____

_____

1 Thessalonians 1:2–3: _____

_____

2 Thessalonians 1:3–4: _____

_____

2 Timothy 1:3–7: _____

_____

Philemon 1:4–7: _____

_____

What is the reoccurring theme in these verses? _____

_____

_____

What comes to your mind when you think of a great church? Answer honestly.

_____

_____

In our focus passage, Ephesians 1:15–16, Paul had a heart full of thanksgiving for fellow Christians who showed love to others through their faith. What makes a church great? We could write thousands of answers that would be valid, but at the core, we must have love, specifically the supernatural love of Christ for others. Listen to what Paul wrote in Galatians. "You, my brothers, were called to be free. But do not use your freedom to indulge the sinful nature, rather, serve one another in love. The entire law is summed up in a single command: 'Love your neighbor as yourself'" (Galatians 5:13–14). "Carry each other's burdens, and in this way you will fulfill the law of Christ" (Galatians 6:2).

Oh, sisters! We have to love one another! We have to carry one another's burdens, and love each other unconditionally! Our only motive should be to fulfill the law of Christ. When you love like that, you will be thankful and appreciate others who love like that as well. It's a rare and beautiful thing to behold. That's why Paul continued to pray for these fellow believers who served with this supernatural love.

Are you thankful for someone in your life who exhibits the kind of faith and love Paul is referring to?

_____

_____

Do you lack this love for both yourself and for those who surround you?

_____

_____

How can you help your church love more?

_____

_____

Sweet sister, life is hard. There are ups and downs, twists and turns, fear and insecurities. Make sure your ride has Jesus as the shock absorber, and make sure you don't ride alone. Open your heart to love like Jesus, and let someone else raise their hands with you when your knuckles are white from gripping the safety bar. You will be so thankful that you did!

Day 4

Divide and Conquer

Ephesians 1:17–18

As I study and write today, I sit in a hotel room in downtown Jackson, Mississippi. My son is working as a senate page at the Capitol, and my daughter is at home with my husband because she has the flu. We have officially entered the divide-and-conquer stage as parents. Mathematically speaking, there is a divide-and-conquer algorithm for solving difficult problems. You have to divide your math problem into sub-problems in order to solve the algorithm and conquer a solution.

In math, the problem is solved. However, in life, not so much. My family may have divided this week, but we definitely have not conquered. My little girl is at home sick and wants her momma. Thankfully, when the algorithm of my week's plan does not have a conquering solution, I am reminded that my King has not only gone before me and conquered this week but that He has conquered it *all*!

We try so hard sometimes to solve life's problems ourselves. We seek answers from a variety of sources.

Where do you turn for answers the most? _____

_____

We long to know God in a deeper, more intimate relationship. Do you know Him? Really know Him? Explain. _____

_____

If you long to know Him better, what is holding you back? _____

_____

Read Ephesians 1:17 and write it here. _____

_____

_____

Read 1 Thessalonians 5:17, Philippians 4:6, and Romans 12:12.

Paul "keeps asking." Paul prays "without ceasing."

Prayer is to our spiritual lives as breathing is to our bodies. A constant state of prayer should become as natural as breathing. But in order for our prayer lives to become this way, we must understand it's an attitude, not a duty. It is constant communication with our Father, who already knows our hearts and minds. Prayer should be our first response to everything we face in a day—fear, anxiety, decisions, praise. We are to come to Him continually, not just in a formal prayer time that we set aside.

God is the source of all we need. He has blessings readily available, but they must be received.

Warren Wiersbe tells the following story of William Randolph Hearst:

William Randolph Hearst was a billionaire who made his fortune as a newspaper publisher. He decided at one point in his life to invest his fortune in great works of art. One day he read about a very valuable piece of art in an art magazine, and he decided that he wanted to buy it. So he called his agent and sent him all over the world trying to find it. The agent searched for it all over the world, but he couldn't find it.

William Randolph Hearst insisted that he find the piece of art; so he sent him out again. Finally, the agent returned and said, "Mr. Hearst, I have found the valuable piece of art you have been searching for."

Mr. Hearst said, "That is wonderful. Where was it?"

The agent said, "It was in your own warehouse, sir. You bought it several years ago."[7]

Christians spend an enormous amount of time searching and seeking blessings. Our problem is not that we lack blessings. It's our lack of understanding when it comes to blessings. We need to stop aimlessly searching and start fervently asking.

Paul's prayer for the Ephesians in Ephesians 1:17 was for them to gain access to the blessings available to them. To know Him better, the Ephesians needed the same blessings we need today.

1. Wisdom

Wisdom can be defined as having discernment or insight. Discernment is the "ability to judge well; obtaining spiritual direction and understanding."[8]

Sign me up, please!

When I teach the topic of wisdom to children, I explain it to them as the ability to know right from wrong. I also tell them they are never too young to be wise or ask for wisdom. It is a blessing for all. God will give it to us in the doses we need. No more, no less.

Read James 1:5 and Colossians 2:3.

Have you asked God for your portion of wisdom? _____

2. Revelation

Merriam-Webster's defines revelation as follows: "an art of revealing or communicating divine truth; something that is revealed by God to humans."[9]

Read Deuteronomy 29:29.

What belongs to us?_____

_____

Read Galatians 1:11–12.

What is Paul explaining? _____

_____

"The Spirit of wisdom of revelation" is not exclusive to some Christians. It's available for all Christians "so that you may know Him better" (Ephesians 1:17).

What does your prayer life look like?_____

_____

What do you pray for most? _____

_____

What can we learn from Paul's prayer life?_____

_____

Read Ephesians 1:18–19.

I want you to imagine for a moment that you get to go on the trip of a lifetime. You arrive in Greece and go to a quaint hotel room. The room is surrounded in walls of curtains. Behind those curtains there is a sweeping, extensive, panoramic view of the glorious Mediterranean Sea. Beyond the curtains there is the most scenic views of the country that anyone has ever seen. You dreamed about the view, and it's right behind the curtains.

Only … you never open them. You wonder what could be behind them. You know it's got to be good, but you choose not to open them. So you do not see, and you never even realize that it's the best view you could ever witness.

The access we have to God can't even be described in words. If we allow Him to "open the eyes of our heart" (Ephesians 1:18), we gain a supernatural glimpse that can't be seen with physical eyes. It's an enlightening vision that allows us to be spiritually aware. The enemy provides curtain after curtain into our minds, which blocks the eyes of our hearts. But God can throw those curtains back if we allow Him.

Do you feel blinded spiritually?

What has He called us to? (Ephesians 1:18). _____

_____

The opposite of hope is despair. In Him we are called to hope. Our hope is Him. Notice the last part of verse 18. *We* are His inheritance!

Did you get that? He loves us so much that He considers us an inheritance to Him.

"His divine power has given us everything we need for a godly life through our knowledge of him who called us by his own glory and goodness. Through these he has given us his very great and precious promises, so that through them you may participate in the divine nature, having escaped the corruption in the world caused by evil desires" (2 Peter 1:3–4).

What does that verse mean to you? _____

_____

My prayer for you today is that you will realize (if you didn't before) that wisdom, revelation, enlightenment, and hope are precious gifts from our Father that are waiting for you.

Day 5

Incomparable Power
Ephesians 1:19–23

Read Ephesians 1:19–23.

The same "incomparably great power" is within those who believe is the power that allowed Jesus Christ to rise from the dead. The same matchless, unparalleled, unrivaled, unequaled, incomparable power is *within* those who believe.

Jesus Christ was raised from the dead, seated at the right hand, and put above all rulers and authorities and dominions. That's the power of Jesus Christ. There are no words to adequately explain.

So what does all this mean for us? _____

_____

Do you truly believe that power lives within you? _____

Read Acts 1:8.
What will you receive? _____

_____

When? _____

Don't let the enemy convince you that the power is weaker just because it's in you. We may be weak on our own, but God's power within us is strong.

God allows difficulties in our lives for many reasons. In our weakness, His power is made stronger.

Read 2 Corinthians 12:7–10.

What did Paul say was the reason for "a thorn in my flesh?" _____

_____

Where did his thorn come from? _____

How many times did Paul plead to God to take it away? _____

How did God answer Paul's prayer? _____

_____

What conclusion did Paul realize? _____

_____

The generality of Paul's thorn is so we can all relate to Paul. Whatever difficulty it is that we face—emotional, physical, spiritual, or financial—there is a purpose for God allowing it in our lives. His grace is sufficient, and His power is made perfect in our weakness.

"His incomparably great power for us who believe" (Ephesians 1:19).

Read Ephesians 1:20–21 again.

We should take great comfort and solace in knowing that no matter who holds any government office, Jesus is King over them all!

Read Ephesians 1:22–23 again.

We will discuss and study more about the church body in chapter 4.

Pray for your church. Pray for the staff and leaders. Pray that Jesus is truly over everything...over *everything*.

Week 2

Day 1

The Darkness of Sin and the Light of Grace

Ephesians 2:1–8

When my children were toddlers, I did not teach them to throw tantrums. You know, the classic lying down on the floor, kicking and screaming in defiance because they are not getting what they want. Then they stop kicking when you try to pick them up. They become stiff and somehow heavier than their little bodies should be. No, I did not teach them that, yet they both did it. We are born with a sinful nature passed down to us from Adam.

Read Romans 5:12.

What entered the world through one man? _____

What entered the world through sin? _____

What came to all men as a result? _____

Who has sinned? _____

Read Ephesians 2:1–3.

What jumps out the most to you in these verses?_____

_____

I must confess that I have read these three passages over and over, praying for God to speak through them to me. They are dark and dreary. So is sin.

Look back at Ephesians 2:2.

What is the kingdom of the air? _____

_____

Since we are born with this sinful nature and since it was passed down to us through Adam, what do we do? _____

_____

Read Romans 5:19–21.

"But where sin increased, _____ increased all the more."

In verse 21, what reigns through righteousness to bring eternal life through Jesus Christ?

_____

Read Ephesians 2:4–8.

What do these verses mean to you? _____

_____

Sin equals death, *but* where sin increased, grace increased more. Sin equals death, *but* because God loves us so much, His grace gives life.

The role of a conjunction in a sentence is to provide clarity for the reader about the subject. Without them, the meaning of the sentence is incomplete or unclear. Sin leaves us dead. Sin wipes out the blessings in our life. But God is real, and so is His grace.

A conjunction changes a sentence. The conjunction *but* in these scriptures changes everything.

Read Romans 6:1–4, Titus 2:11–14, and Ephesians 2:8. Write down your thoughts from these verses. _____

_____

_____

What is our gift from God? _____

_____

We do not deserve grace. It is a free gift from God. Do not allow sin to cover your life in darkness. Just as a toddler has to learn to be obedient, so do we as Christians.

"Do not conform any longer to the pattern of this world, but be transformed by the renewing of your mind. Then you will be able to test and approve what God's will is – His good, pleasing and perfect will" (Romans 12:2).

Day 2

God's Workmanship

Ephesians 2:9-10

Read Ephesians 2:9–10.

In verse 9, what does "so that no one can boast" mean? _____

_____

Read verse 8 again. What is our gift? _____

_____

*I*magine the mayhem of Christianity if we could boast our way into heaven. False religions teach that you must earn your way to heaven with works. Our salvation is a gift. The price was paid in full by the blood of our Savior. All we must do is accept that beautiful gift.

If you have received that beautiful gift, you, my dear, are sealed in with salvation. But are you using that gift to further the kingdom?

Read James 2:14–26.

Why was Abraham considered righteous? _____

_____

Why was Rahab considered righteous? _____

_____

"As the body without the spirit is dead, so faith without deeds is dead" (James 2:26).

Let's speak in a language I know best—coffee. If someone gave you a barista-style coffee maker as a gift and you accepted that gift, Girl, you have *the* coffee maker. But if you don't read the manual and use the coffee maker to fill your cup and the cups of others, what good is it?

Read James 2:20.

What is faith without deeds? _____

_____

It's useless, my friends. Oh, and it's foolish. I really don't want to be useless or foolish. Do you?

While in Jackson, I had a beautiful view outside my hotel window of the downtown area. I have always loved the rich history and architecture of old downtowns. One particular building from this view caught my eye immediately. It was a beautiful tall brick building with a rather large marque on top that read, "Standard Life." The architecture intrigued me, so I did a little research on the building.

The Standard Life Building was built in 1929 by New Orleans architect Claude Lindsey. Originally known as the Tower Building, it was constructed for office space in downtown Jackson after the Great Depression in the hopes that it would attract more businesses to the area. At the time it was built, it was the largest concrete building in the world and the tallest building in Jackson. A beacon light was added at the top that was said to flash a beam for fifty miles, illuminating the Vicksburg bridge. In the *Jackson Daily News* in 1929, an article was published that said the building would have an underground passageway connecting to the Edward's Hotel (where I was staying).

It was quite fascinating to say the least! So why would a building so majestic with such rich history and architecture be adorned with a marque with the words "Standard Life?" The building is anything but standard.

What labels do you put on yourself? _____

_____

What labels do you put on others? _____

_____

Read Ephesians 2:10.

Why would we ever lessen ourselves to be anything but the work of art we are? We're God's workmanship!

What lies about ourselves do we believe? _____

_____

Read Genesis 1:27 and 2 Corinthians 5:17.

What do those verses mean to you? _____

_____

You are God's masterpiece, created in His image. And when you accept the gift of salvation, you become a new creation in Him.

Compare your spiritual journey to that of the metamorphosis of a caterpillar to a butterfly:

_____

_____

Read Ephesians 2:10 again, focusing on what we were created to do. We were created to do good works. And God prepared them in what ways?

_____

_____

Read Jeremiah 1:5. What did God tell Jeremiah? _____

_____

Before we were even born, God knew what He could accomplish through us. We will specifically discuss doing good works with spiritual gifts in chapter 4.

I close today with Revelation 3:2, which says, "Wake up! Strengthen what remains and is about to die, for I have not found your deeds complete in the sight of My God."

Pray that God will show you what you need to complete life with pure motives.

Day 3

One in Christ

Ephesians 2:11–19

*T*oday we will cover the uniting power of Jesus Christ's blood. Salvation was and is offered to all people.

Read Genesis 17:1–14.

What was the sign of the covenant? _____

_____

In biblical days you were either a Jew or a Gentile. Jews were followers of God that followed covenant laws. Gentiles were followers of pagan gods.

Fast-forward to the New Testament. Jesus changed everything.

Read Acts 15:1–12.

The covenant was still in debate at the Jerusalem council in this passage. Imagine the scene here with these godly men—Paul, Barnabas, Peter, and James. What was on their hearts in this debate? What were they trying to make the Jewish leaders understand? _____

_____

Read Ephesians 2:11–13.

In verse 11, Paul explains that the covenantal act of circumcision was done by "the hands of _____" (NIV).

What do you think is the deeper meaning here? _____

_____

In verse 12, what were the former Gentiles excluded from? _____

_____

What changed for them in verse 13? _____

_____

Read Ephesians 2:14–19.
"He came and preached peace to you who were far away and peace to those who were near" (Ephesians 2:17).
Gentiles were "far off" from God. Jews were "nigh" or "near" (almost) to God.
The gospel brought everyone to the same access and love.
Read Matthew 27:50–51.
What happened when Jesus died? _____

_____

Read Hebrews 9:1–7.
Who could enter the inner room? _____

_____

Read Ephesians 2:18.
What does everyone now have through Him? _____

_____

Access is "a means of approaching or entering a place; entrance, entry, way in, approach."[10]
Gentiles could only become followers of God in the Old Testament by adhering to the covenant. Jews had a covenant and acceptance through law and sacrifice. Neither had access. Jesus changed everything. And that access is offered to everyone.
What word is mentioned four times in Ephesians 2:14–17? _____

Why was this so important in these passages? _____

_____

God "destroyed the barrier" between Himself and man.
The blood of Jesus destroyed the old covenants and old laws that required flesh and made the relationship a matter of the heart!

Day 4

Foundations, Cornerstones, and Rocks

Ephesians 2:19–22

Foundations

Read Ephesians 2:19–22.

What was God's household built on?_____

_____

A foundation is the basis or groundwork of anything.

Before the Gentiles converted to Christianity, they were building on false religions. The Jews were busying themselves with building on strict religious traditions and law. Neither of these were firm foundations. Yet before Christ, it was the groundwork and base of their entire spirituality.

In Ephesians 2:20, Paul points out the apostles and the prophets who took part in laying this foundation. They declared New Testament truth when they were filled with the Holy Spirit.

Read Matthew 7:24–27.

Explain what these verses in Matthew mean to you. _____

_____

A builder knows that the foundation is the most important part of building a house. The right mixture of strong soils underneath the foundation is crucial. If the foundation is not laid correctly, everything else built upon it will be *off*, which, in turn, will make the whole building less stable. This could cause windows and walls to crack, doors to be misaligned, gaps to develop between the wall and ceiling, and water to seep in, and worst-case scenario, the building could collapse.

The same is true of our spiritual foundation. Just as a beautiful house cannot fake a poor foundation, we can't either. The cracks and misalignments always surface.

Is your foundation strong?

Cornerstones

Read Ephesians 2:20.

Who is the chief cornerstone? _____

A cornerstone can be described in this way: "The cornerstone (or foundation stone) concept is derived from the first stone set in the construction of a masonry foundation, important since all other stones will be set in reference to this stone, thus determining the position of the entire structure."[11]

Is Jesus your cornerstone?

Does He set the reference that determines everything in your life?

Read Psalm 118:22, Matthew 21:42, Mark 12:10, Luke 20:17, Acts 4:11, and 1 Peter 2:7.

What do these verses say? _____

_____

_____

In ancient days, highly trained stonemasons would choose stones from a quarry (a large pit where stone was extracted). The cornerstone was the most important stone chosen. Masons would inspect many stones before choosing the perfect cornerstone. This meant they rejected many stones that they could use for later building.

Jesus was rejected on earth by Jewish builders of religion, but He is the cornerstone of our salvation. He joined both Jew and Gentile together. On the cross at His death, He joined God the Father, God the Son, and God the Spirit.

He is the Cornerstone.

Rocks and Stones

Read Ephesians 2:21–22.

What is Paul referring to in verse 21 as the "whole building?" _____

_____

What is the significance of verse 22? _____

_____

Paul envisioned the church as a building that would continue to grow—the kind of church growth that was described by Luke in Acts.

Read a few of the following verses (or all of them): Acts 2:41, 47; 5:14; 6:1, 7; 11:21; 14:1; 17:12, 34; 18:8; and 19:10.

Where God used to only be found in a physical temple, He now abides in the believer. When we accept Him, we now have full access as He dwells in us—the living temple.

Read 1 Peter 2:4–12.

What are we referred to? _____

What are we being built into? _____

Rocks and stones play an important role throughout history. We are about to embark on a geology lesson. If God created nature—and we know He did—don't you think there are countless messages and so much knowledge throughout everything He created? What are we to learn from the details of a flower? A weed? The rings in a tree? Is it useless information? I don't think so.

Dig deep into anything God created, and you'll find Him. Just as an artist has meaning in what he or she paints, God, the ultimate artist, does too.

Really think about your spiritual walk as we study some geology. If you would have ever told me that I would be studying geology and enjoying it, I would have definitely laughed. We put God in a box, and we expect Him to speak to us in certain ways. Expect the unexpected.

Over the course of time, rocks can *transform* from one type into another. This process is called the rock cycle. If rocks are called to be transformed and obey, don't you think our calling is even higher than that of a rock? Rocks do not stay the same!

"Do not conform any longer to the pattern of this world, but be transformed by the renewing of your mind. Then you will be able to test and approve what God's will is; His good, pleasing and perfect will" (Romans 12:2).

"And we, who with unveiled faces all reflect the Lord's glory, are being transformed into His likeness with ever increasing glory, which comes from the Lord, who is the Spirit" (2 Corinthians 3:18).

Three General Classes of Rock

A. Igneous

The Latin word *igneous* means "of fire." This type of rock forms when lava cools and becomes solid. The melting of rocks is caused by one or more of three processes, namely (1) an increase in temperature, (2) a decrease in pressure, or (3) a change in composition.

As living stones, we should

- increase in temperature (i.e., being on fire for God),
- decrease in pressure (i.e., freeing ourselves from worldly things that consume), and
- undergo a change in composition (i.e., changing our attitudes to be more like Christ).

Consider *fire*. "'Is not my word like fire,' declares the Lord, 'and like a hammer that breaks a rock into pieces?'" (Jeremiah 23:29).

Consider *pressure*. "But godliness with contentment is great gain. For we brought nothing into the world and we can take nothing out of it" (1 Timothy 6:6–7).

Consider *Attitudes*. "To be made new in the attitude of your minds" (Ephesians 4:23). "And to put on the new self, created to be like God in true righteousness and holiness" (Ephesians 4:24).

B. Sedimentary

These rocks are a melting pot of particles from other rocks that have compacted together, particles from rocks that over the years have been weathered and eroded, particles that have been moved all over by wind, water, ice, among other forces. These broken pieces are cemented together.

Think of our community and our church. While some people are igneous (on fire), others are broken, weathered, eroded, hurt, scattered about by life, waiting to be cemented back together.

"But those who hope in the Lord will renew their strength. They will soar on wings like eagles; they will run and not grow weary, they will walk and not be faint" (Isaiah 40:31).

God takes the broken pieces and puts them back together! Oh my!

C. Metamorphic

When rocks are exposed to different temperatures or pressures, they are altered.

So through the process of metamorphism, an old rock can be changed into something completely new (e.g., marble, quartz, slate). It can become something beautiful and useful.

"Therefore, if anyone is in Christ, the new creation has come: The old has gone, the new is here!" (2 Corinthians 5:17).

Are you allowing what you are going through to change you into something beautiful and useful for His kingdom?

God cares so much more about His living stones!

Read 1 Peter 2:5 again.

Read Ephesians 2:22 again.

Several years ago I had a dream that was so real that it still gives me goose bumps. For months it was all I could think about. This was the dream.

One night before bed, I walked outside and looked up at the sky. (I often do this. I love a clear night to see the stars.). As I looked, the clouds and stars began to swirl and mix together before my eyes. I ran into the house and got Jay. When we both looked back up at the sky, symbols carved on stone filled the sky. We stared in disbelief for quite some time. Jay asked, "What does it mean?"

I remember being deep in thought in the dream, wanting to write the message down. I knew even in my dream it was a message from God. Then … I woke up.

Not long after this dream, I began to dig deeper in the word. Foundations, cornerstones, stone and rock studying began. Things in His Word began to make more sense, and it made me want to dig even deeper. And this is where *Ephesians* began.

Friends, He has a message for all of us in His Word. What doesn't seem clear can become clear. What seems like a foreign language can become one you completely understand. Do not stop your studying. Listen to Him. He has so much He wants you to know.

Let's close today with Hebrews 11:10. Let God build you into the temple you were always meant to be.

Day 5

Ephesians 2

Read back through the entire chapter 2 of Ephesians.

Ask God to teach you something new.

What spoke to you the most from this chapter? _____

_____

_____

_____

Day 1

For This Reason ...

Ephesians 3:1–13

Read Ephesians 3:1.

Who does Paul say he is a prisoner of?_____

_____

Why do you think Paul refers to his imprisonment this way (instead of saying "a prisoner of the Jews")? _____

_____

This verse reminds me how important it is to read all scriptures, not skipping over anything. It all has life and meaning. Each time I've taken a portion of Ephesians to study, I pray that God will help me not only understand but also see how to relate it to my life and how to teach it. There have been many times when it's taken me a while to *get it*. But when those moments arise, we have to press on and allow God to reveal things to us in His time. If we don't, we might miss the meaning altogether.

In verse 1 in an ever-so-subtle message that speaks volumes, we see that Paul does not refer to himself as a prisoner of the Jews but as a "prisoner of Christ Jesus." I could have skipped over this verse easily, but it stuck out to me.

Paul's attitude is always on point. His wisdom always shines through his circumstances. He knows God is always in control. Listen to what John MacArthur Jr. has to say about this particular verse.

> Perspective is all-important. How we view and react to circumstances is more important than the circumstances themselves. IF all we can see is our immediate situation, then our circumstances control us. We

41

feel good when our circumstances are good but miserable when they are not. Had Paul been able to see only his circumstances, he would quickly have given up his ministry. Had he thought that his life was ultimately in the hands of his persecutors, his jailers, his guards, or the Roman government, he would long since have given up in despair. But Paul's perspective was a divine perspective, and he lived with total trust in God's purposes. It was not that he himself knew his future or fully understood the divine purposes behind his afflictions, but he knew that his future, his afflictions, and every other aspect of his life was totally in his Lord's hands.[12]

Wow! Just wow! Paul knew that every circumstance should be lived out for the cause of Christ. He always clearly realized that time should never be wasted. Instead of wallowing in self-pity from the unfairness of being wrongly imprisoned, he penned Ephesians.

What circumstances are you facing right now? Are your circumstances consuming you? Are you allowing them to consume you for Christ?_____

_____

_____

I often tell my children that how we react to situations can often be more important than the situation itself.

Paul's ministry was full of self-sacrifice and service. He knew his imprisonment was for the sake of the Gentiles and ultimately, the sake of Christ.

Are you involved in any selfless service? _____

What happens when our ministries or our service become about ourselves?_____

_____

Read Ephesians 3:2–6.
Describe the mystery that Paul is talking about. _____

_____

_____

Refer back to Ephesians 1:17. What prayer did Paul have? What word sticks out to you that are also mentioned in 3:3? _____

_____

_____

Paul spends some time in these verses, reviewing them to the Gentiles. He reminds them of the apostolic position the Lord has given him in order to bring the message of the gospel to them. He reminds them that they are "heirs together with Israel, members together of one body, and sharers together in the promise in Christ Jesus" (Ephesians 3:6).

Read Ephesians 3:7–9.

How did Paul become a servant of the gospel? _____

_____

Read 1 Corinthians 15:9–10, 1 Timothy 1:15, and Ephesians 3:8.

What is the common thread in these verses? _____

_____

Instead of Paul boasting that God has given him such revelation into the mystery, he remained humble. Paul knew that it was only by God's grace alone that he was allowed to be a servant of Christ.

Do you struggle with being humble?

Read the following verses and make notes by each one. I know this seems like a lot of Bible pages to flip through, but trust me on the importance of this exercise. We all struggle with at least one of these topics about the lack of humility. If we are honest, we struggle with more than one too. Pray as you read so that God will make it clear where your struggle lies.

Philippians 2:3: _____

_____

Proverbs 11:2: _____

_____

Romans 12:16: _____

_____

1 Peter 3:3–4: _____

_____

James 4:10: _____

_____

Colossians 3:12: _____

_____

Proverbs 22:4: _____

_____

1 Peter 5:6: _____

_____

James 3:13: _____

_____

Matthew 6:2: _____

_____

Galatians 5:13: _____

_____

These, my friends, are just a few verses that declare humility. It is of the utmost importance to God that we remain humble in spirit.

Read Ephesians 3:10–13.

Throughout the first part of chapter 3, Paul is leading up to a prayer for the Ephesians.

How does verse 12 make you feel? _____

_____

We close today with Ephesians 3:13, which says, "I ask you, therefore, not to be discouraged because of my sufferings for you, which are your glory."

Paul knew that it would be hard for some to get past the fact he was in prison. His situation from an earthly perspective looked grim. Paul's reminder to not become discouraged can be applied to any circumstance we face today.

Read the following verses and write them down.

2 Thessalonians 3:13: _____

_____

Galatians 6:9: _____

_____

Philippians 4:9: _____

_____

Whatever season you are in, do not be discouraged. Do not allow your circumstances to consume you. Allow God to use your present situation to bring Him glory.

Day 2

A Prayer for the Ephesians-Part 1

Ephesians 3:14–16

$\mathcal{E}$phesians 3:14–21 is the prayer that Paul has been leading up to from the first verse in chapter 3.

Read Ephesians 3:14–15.

When was the last time you kneeled in prayer?_____

_____

I pray in the car, in the bed, in the shower, and loading the dishwasher. But there is something very special about my prayer time when I kneel. For me, when I take the time to kneel before the Lord in prayer, it is intentional and purposeful. It is a time that seems less hurried and less distracted.

In Old Testament days, kneeling and bowing were customary practices that were done before a king. Kneeling was a sign of reverence and submission. Bowing was a sign of respect or gratitude.

Read Luke 22:39–42.

Jesus kneeled in prayer in full submission to the Father.

Read Matthew 6:5–13.

Jesus made it clear in scripture that either kneeling or standing, our prayer should be from the heart.

Read Ephesians 3:15, which says, "From whom his whole family in heaven and on earth derives its name."

The word *family* here is translated from the Greek and can also mean fatherhood.

God is the Father of all fathers. I'm not sure what your relationship on earth with your earthly father has been like. But you can rest assured the Father of all fathers loves you with a love that is not comparable to anything on earth.

So Paul is kneeling before the Father of all fathers in prayer.

Read Ephesians 3:16.
What does this verse mean to you? _____

_____

Paul is praying for the Lord to "strengthen you with power ... out of glorious riches." God's riches are limitless, and His power and strength are incomprehensible.

Where do you find your strength? _____

_____

Many years ago I learned that my lower back problems were due to a weak core. Your core muscles are the most important group of muscles in your body. If your core muscles are weak or inadequate, you can suffer from poor posture, serious back problems, weak stability and balance, and overall muscle weakness. So personal trainers will tell you to strengthen your core.

The same is true of our spiritual walk. Paul's prayer was for the Lord to "strengthen you with power through his Spirit in your inner being" (Ephesians 3:16).

Read the following verses on strength and make notes about which ones speak to you right now.

Psalm 22:19: _____

_____

Psalm 28:7–8: _____

_____

Psalm 46:1: _____

_____

Psalm 119:28: _____

_____

Isaiah 33:2: _____

_____

Isaiah 40:29: _____

_____

Isaiah 40:31: _____

_____

Habakkuk 3:19: _____

_____

2 Corinthians 12:9–10: _____

_____

Philippians 4:13: _____

_____

Find your strength from the source.

Day 3

A Prayer for the Ephesians-Part 2

Rooted
Ephesians 3:17–19

Read Ephesians 3:17–19.

What are the specific details of Paul's prayer? _____

_____

The livelihood and health of a tree depend on its root system. What you see above ground is dependent upon what's underneath. Healthy roots provide nutrients and store water. Healthy roots stabilize a tree, acting as an anchor. And as we all know, trees must have water, good soil, and light in order to grow. Plants and trees know their source. Roots will stretch to find water. And a plant will reach for light in the direction the sun shines. And without a foundation of good soil, a plant or tree will never take root.

We, too, must know our source of strength to grow in a firm foundation of good soil, drink from the living water, and look to our source of light.

Good Soil as Our Foundation to Grow

Read Ezekiel 17:8 and Matthew 13:23.
Is the Word of God able to take root and grow in your life right now? _____

_____

Drink from the Living Water

Read John 4:14 and 7:38.
Are you drinking from the only water that will satisfy? _____

_____

Our Source of Light

Read John 8:12 and 1 John 1:5.
Are you allowing the light of the world to shine through your darkness? _____

_____

Roots can be deep, shallow, or exposed. What type of root system do you think you have? _____

Deep Roots

Once a taproot grows from a seedling, a tree's root system can spread, providing a good solid anchor and a vast source of nutrient intake. The stronger the roots, the wider the outstretched branches, which thus produces more foliage, oxygen, and fruit.
Read Jeremiah 17:8, Ezekiel 31:3–7, Romans 11:16, Psalm 1:3, Colossians 2:6–7, and John 15:5.
Which verse means the most to you? _____

_____

The deeper our roots in Christ, the wider our branches and fruit are to the kingdom of God.
Are your roots deep enough to produce outstretched branches and fruit? What should this look like for a deeply rooted Christian? _____

_____

Shallow Roots

Roots that are shallow are close to the surface and not very deep. These roots can be easily damaged and become a nuisance for yard work, sidewalks, and driveways. Trees that have shallow roots can be easily uprooted, and they won't survive a storm.

Read Matthew 15:13, Mark 4:5–7, and Luke 8:11–15.

Are your roots in Christ shallow (surface level) or strong? _____

Exposed Roots

Trees that have visibly exposed roots were either poorly planted or didn't have sufficient space to grow. Exposed roots can also be caused by soil erosion, heavy rain, or wind. Roots that are exposed can be easily damaged.

Read Mark 4:17 and Revelation 3:15–16.

A faulty root system that was poorly planted will eventually be exposed. A lukewarm Christian's shallow roots will also one day be exposed. You can't fake strong roots.

Do you know without a doubt that you are firmly planted and rooted in Christ?

Are you allowing things of this world to crowd out the space for you to grow in Christ?

Settle it today, my sister.

Paul's prayer in Ephesians 3:17–19 is for us to not only be rooted in Christ but to also be rooted in love and to know that Christ's love for us is vaster and deeper than we could ever comprehend.

Does knowing how much God loves you help you love others?

Read the following verses about God calling us to love: Proverbs 10:12; Matthew 5:44; 22:37–39; John 13:34–35; Romans 12:10; 1 Corinthians 13:3; 1 Peter 4:8; and 1 John 4:7–8.

Read the following verses about how much God's love is for us: Psalm 103:8;

Lamentations 3:22–23; John 3:16; Romans 5:8; 8:38–39; Galatians 2:20; and 1 John 4:19.

Paul knew that for the church to thrive, they had to not only know how much God loved them but also demonstrate that love for others.

As we close today, read Ephesians 3:19 again, "To be filled to the measure of all the fullness of God."

Plant your roots deep, sister. Let your branches spread wide with love for others in and outside of the church, bearing fruit in vast abundance as Christ spread His arms wide on the cross in love for us. Let the storms of life only sway you gently as your roots in Christ anchor your faith deeply. Drink from the living water and reach for the source of true light in a dark world. Grow strong and flourish, my friend. And know how much your Father loves you.

Corrie Ten Boom said, "There is no pit so deep that God's love is not deeper still."[13]

Day 4

A Prayer for the Ephesians–Part 3

God's Power within Us
Ephesians 3:20–21

We are at the closing verses of Paul's prayer to the Ephesians. And while the closing consists of only two verses, they are full of wisdom, insight, and praise.
Read Ephesians 3:20–21.
Let's focus on verse 20 for a minute. What does this verse mean to you? _____

_____

_____

God's power is limitless and immeasurable. God is *able* to do all that we *ask* or *think* or *imagine*. Our prayers are not always answered in the way we desire them to be. God takes a request on the behalf of a believer and is "able to do above and beyond all that we asked for or thought" (Ephesians 3:20). Paul experienced this over and over with the Lord.
Read Romans 1:8–13.
In these verses, what can we clearly read that Paul wanted to do? _____

_____

Paul planted evangelistic churches. He wanted to go to Rome, where a thriving church already existed, but he was prevented at the time. Had he gone to Rome and taught what he wanted to teach, we would not have Romans. God knew Paul wanted to physically go to Rome. God took Paul's request and was "able to do above and beyond" what Paul could have ever even dreamed (Ephesians 3:20). Paul's letter to the Romans is still alive and relevant today, working miracles in people's lives.

Look back at the last part of Ephesians 3:20.

Where is God's power at work? _____

_____

First and foremost, make sure that you have sealed your salvation in the Lord. If God is not Lord over your life, His power cannot be at work within you. Do *not* be afraid to secure that with Him. Do *not* be afraid or embarrassed to talk with someone if you are unsure. You may have attended church your entire life traditionally and never made this decision.

Believers, are you in any way hindering God's power? Are you allowing, submitting, and yielding to God's power that is at work within you?

_____

_____

Imagine what we miss out on within the kingdom of the Lord when we choose not to submit to the power of God.

Are we spending more time building our kingdom on earth or God's kingdom in heaven?

_____

Read 1 Corinthians 3:9–15.

What materials are you using to build upon the foundation of Jesus Christ? _____

_____

When the world is over, the church will be raptured. The judgment of all Christians will come. Our motives will be exposed, and rewards will be given to believers. Our work on earth will be "shown for what it is" (1 Corinthians 3:13). If what we have built on earth escapes fire, we will be rewarded. If what we have built on earth does not last ("if it is burned up" as indicated 1 Corinthians 3:15), we will *not* lose our salvation, but we will have only escaped hell and not have heavenly eternal rewards.

Are you building on the foundation of Jesus Christ (the cornerstone)? Are you allowing God's power within you to bring God glory?

Gold, silver, and costly stones will last forever. Ask yourself the following questions:

- Are you discipling others?
- Are you serving in your church?
- Does your life reflect Jesus Christ?
- Are your motives pure?

Write 1 Peter 1:7. _____

_____

_____

Wood, hay, and straw will not survive the fire. Ask yourself the following questions:

- Are you more concerned with life on earth than eternal life?
- Are you too busy to serve others?
- Do you work hard for money to use on just yourself or your family?

Write Matthew 6:19. _____

_____

_____

Allow God's power to work within you. Expect Him to do great things through you. Read Ephesians 3:21.

God should always get the credit, the honor, the glory, and the praise when He does a mighty work through us.

We can do nothing on our own, but we can do "all things through Christ who gives us strength" (Philippians 4:13).

Give credit where credit is due. It's our human nature to desire praise, glory, and honor. If you struggle with this, take it to the King. And know you will be rewarded in due time.

Let's close today with Revelation 4:11.

Day 5

Review

go back through days 1 through 4.

What verses in Ephesians 3 stood out to you the most? _____

_____

_____

_____

Did God reveal something new to you? _____

_____

_____

What can you apply to your life right now that you learned in chapter 3? _____

_____

_____

What would be a prayer to your church? Write it below.

_____

_____

_____

Week 4

Day 1

A Life Worthy of the Calling

Ephesians 4:1–6

In Ephesians 4, Paul will address the importance and vitality of unity in the body of Christ, the church. What is your individual role in the church? Is it really that important? Can you be strong in the Lord without being a part of a church?

Read Ephesians 4:1.

Once again, Paul refers to himself as a prisoner of the Lord. We studied the reasons for this on day 1 of week 3. See those notes.

Write what you think Paul means when he says, "I urge you to live a life worthy of the calling." _____

_____

Our lives should be lived in a way that brings glory and honor to the Lord in every way. God deserves that from us, don't you think?

Do you live a life that is worthy of the calling? At work? With your friends? When disagreements arise? At your child's ball game? At church?

Write in your own words how you would define character. _____

_____

_____

The Cambridge Dictionary defines character as "the particular combination of things about a person, especially things you cannot see, that make that person different from others."[14] *The Macmillan Dictionary* defines character as "the qualities that makeup someone's personality."[15] Synonyms for character are essence, identity, disposition, mentality, temperament, nature, personality, and properties.[16]

How would you define your character? _____

_____

How would others define your character? _____

_____

Does your character reflect a life worthy of the calling?

I've always told my children that your character is who you really are when no one but God can see.

Read Ephesians 4:2.

What qualities does Paul mention in these verses that our lives should reflect?

1. Humble (NIV) and Lowliness (KJV)

"Do nothing from selfish ambition or conceit, but in humility count others more significant than yourselves. Let each of you look not only to his own interests, but also to the interests of others" (Philippians 2:3–4).

Are you humble in spirit? _____

2. Gentle (NIV) and Meekness (KJV)

Keep in mind that meek does not mean weak.

"Blessed are the meek, for they will inherit the earth" (Matthew 5:5).

Are you gentle to others? When conflict arises, are you meek? Or do you argue and quarrel to prove a point? Do you have self-control?

Biblically speaking, meekness is "strength under control" (as Abraham Lincoln stated in his poem "Meekness Is Not Weakness").

3. Patient (NIV) and Long-suffering (KJV)

Bearing with one another in love (NIV)   Forbearing one another in love (KJV)

"Love is patient, love is kind. It does not envy, it does not boast, it is not proud" (1 Corinthians 13:4).

Are you patient in love with others? Are you able to endure (long-suffering) hardships or offenses?

Do you exhibit those qualities of character as a church member?

Sometimes we are the harshest to our church family and staff. But apparently, this is nothing new as Paul was addressing this at the very beginning of his charge in order to build unity in the body of Christ.

Is it because we have church leaders and faithful members who serve so high on pedestals that their fall is more drastic? Is it because we expect near perfection from believers? Are we less patient with our church family because they should respond with love and be able to take it?

Whatever the reasons we as church members in the body of Christ do this, it's *wrong*!

Read Ephesians 4:3.

What are we supposed to make every effort to keep? _____

Read Ephesians 4:4–6.

There is ultimately one church. Even though there are countless denominations and churches all over, there is only one church. There is one Spirit, one hope, one Lord, one faith, one baptism, one God and Father of all.

Our one hope as believers is the second coming of our Lord.

Let's close today with Colossians 1:10.

Day 2

Gifts and Grace

Ephesians 4:7–13

When I was younger, I had a huge misconception of what spiritual gifts were. This was due in part to many reasons. First, I had truly never taken the time to dig deep in the Word to understand what spiritual gifts really are. Second, I had always heard Christians throw around the words *talents* and *gifts* as if they were the same. So for years I had put spiritual gifts into a tiny box of talents and wondered why I didn't have any. I could not sing, and I couldn't play the piano or any other instrument, so I thought I had just missed the boat. And the enemy wants us to stay on that delusional shore. I could not have been more wrong, more misinformed, or more uneducated (because I didn't pursue study in the area).

My prayer for you is that after today's lesson, you will have more insight into what your spiritual gifts are. My husband wrote his dissertation on spiritual gifts for his doctorate. At the end of today's lesson, you can use a spiritual gifts inventory (compiled by Dr. Jay Cook) to help guide you in determining what your gifts are. (You can download the document at www.drjaycook.com/spiritual-gifts). I pray that God will use it to guide you and show you what He has gifted to you.

Read Ephesians 4:7.

The more gifts God has given us, the more grace we need. God has portioned out the amount of grace and gifts we need as individuals to balance one another. This is not a "one size fits all" or "one size fits most" approach. Clothes that are sized that way have never fit me anyway. There is no other person on the earth who has been portioned the same amount of grace that is measured perfectly and tweaked every second. If that doesn't make you feel special and loved, I'm not sure what will.

Read Ephesians 4:8–10.

In verse 8, Paul is actually quoting the Old Testament. Read Psalm 68:18.

In Psalm 68, David is referring to God conquering enemies, setting His captives free from slavery (Israelites), and Israel being lifted high in power at the time.

Paul quotes this passage in Ephesians to make a point through a comparison. After an earthly king won a battle, he would parade into his homeland in victory and bring gifts for his people from the conquered foe. His captive soldiers were set free. This must have been such an exciting time of victory and celebration.

Our King of Kings, Jesus, conquered a battle over sin and death that set us free from captivity. He ascended into heaven with victory over the grave and lavished gifts and grace among His people.

Read Ephesians 4:9–10 again.

Write what you think Paul means when he says Jesus "descended to the lower earthly region_____

_____

Read 1 Peter 3:18–20.

Who did Jesus preach to? _____

Read Ephesians 4:11–13

What are the five gifts Jesus gave? _____

_____

Why were these gifts given? _____

_____

These five spiritual gifts are given as an umbrella to some in order to equip and guide other Christians to use their spiritual gifts within His church.

The offices of apostle and prophet do not exist anymore because these are not needed. However, the spiritual gifts of prophecy and apostleship are still given today.

The five gifts given in Ephesians 4 are different from the gifts mentioned in 1 Corinthians 12. In Ephesians, the gifts mentioned refer to the universal church as a whole. They trickle down under the umbrella I mentioned to the local church of believers. These gifts are in 1 Corinthians 12.

Read 1 Corinthians 12:4–11 and 12:28.

Write down the spiritual gifts given that are mentioned in 1 Corinthians. _____

_____

_____

These spiritual gifts are thoroughly explained in a document on the same webpage as the inventory of spiritual gifts I previously mentioned (available at www.drjaycook. com/spiritual-gifts).

Read Ephesians 4:12 again.

Now read 1 Corinthians 12:12–31.

Write down 1 Corinthians 12:26–27. _____

_____

_____

_____

Read Romans 12:4–8.

What are the spiritual gifts mentioned in these verses? _____

_____

_____

Clearly, God intended for believers to use their gifts within a local church.

Read Ephesians 4:13.

What do you think this verse means? _____

_____

Our goal as Christians is to become like Christ. Everything we do should be working toward attaining that goal. We want to grow in the fullness of Him.

There are so many believers who have convinced themselves that they should not fully serve or even attend a local church. I've heard so many excuses. "Only hypocrites attend." "I've been hurt too many times." "The Lord hasn't revealed which church I should join." "I can feel close to God on my boat. I don't have to be in church."

And the list goes on and on.

Friends, clearly we have just seen in scripture that we all have an important role in our local church. A portion of grace was designed for you with gifts that fit no one else. Without you, the recipe is off. Do not fool yourselves into thinking this does not apply to you.

John Phillips says,

If an individual believer is to mature fully, he needs the fellowship of other believers. The idea of an arm or a leg developing in isolation from other members of the body is ludicrous. No one can attain full spiritual maturity apart from the give-and-take of a local church fellowship. The New Testament does not mention freelance evangelists, independent missionaries, itinerant Bible teachers, or other Christians who have no local fellowship and are responsible to no one but themselves.[17]

Are you involved in a local church?

Do you know what your gifts are?

What is holding you back?

Please download and complete the spiritual inventory. Pray over it first, and use it as a guide. I pray God will show you your gifts and lead you to use them.

Will you be at risk of failing or getting hurt? Of course! But God is in control, and He knows what He is doing. He will equip you for the task He gives you.

In order to become mature and attain the whole measure of the fullness of Christ, we have to quit picking and choosing what portions of scripture we are going to live out.

Day 3

Progressive Waves

Ephesians 4:14–16

O h, how I love the beach! There's warm sun, a gentle breeze, white sand, and the sound of waves crashing on the shore. But the change in wind and waves can change your day at the beach in an instant. A beach day can be calm, peaceful, and beautiful, or it can be dangerous with undertows, tidal waves, and sand-beating winds. Imagine how the later would change your day at the beach. No matter the condition of the sea at any given moment, the water is always moving—this is, if there is life within.

The same can be said of our local churches and her members. In what direction are you helping your church move in?

An undertow can be deadly if a person gets caught off guard in one. The definition of an undertow is "any strong current below the surface of a body of water, moving in a direction different from that of the surface current."[18]

Have you ever been a part of an undertow within a church? Have you felt a strong current of negativity behind the scenes of a body of believers, one moving in a different direction from the teachings of Christ? You have to have wisdom from God to get out of that sort of undertow unharmed!

Have you ever experienced anything like this? Have you seen it in a church?

Read Ephesians 4:14.

A spiritual infant can be easily swayed, can be tossed back and forth in what they believe, and can easily fall prey to false teachers and an undertow of deceitfulness.

Read 2 Timothy 4:3.

Are you spiritually mature enough to withstand an undertow of this nature? Or will you be swept away by a strong current that goes against the fullness of Christ mentioned in Ephesians 4:13?

Read James 1:5–8.

What do you need to do what is mentioned in these verses? _____

_____

_____

Have you ever heard of progressive waves? They're named *progressive* because they move with a steady speed. One type of progressive wave is a capillary wave, also known as a ripple. For there to be life in water, it has to be constantly moving. Otherwise, it's stagnant. Stagnant water has "no current or flow and often has an unpleasant smell as a consequence."[19]

Read Ephesians 4:15–16.

Think of your role as a church member. Are you like a progressive wave, always moving and serving, keeping peace in the waters? Are you part of the love and fellowship that helps hold things together?

Explain: _____

_____

Or are you like stagnant water with no movement at all?

Remember the verse about being lukewarm? "So, because you are lukewarm … neither hot nor cold … I am about to spit you out of my mouth" (Revelation 3:16).

Don't fool yourself into thinking a ripple in the water doesn't matter. The water is either moving and sustaining life or stagnant with no flow and an unpleasant smell. Which are you? There is no in between.

Day 4

Living in the Light

Ephesians 4:17–24

*I*n a dark room, you cannot see what is right in front of you. In a dim room, you can only see some things. In a room full of light, you see just about everything.
Read Ephesians 4:17–18.
Why must we not be like Gentiles? _____

_____

We must never fool ourselves into thinking an unbeliever will think like a believer. So the next time you receive good advice from an intellectually smart person who just happens to also be an unbeliever, think again! Unbelievers are blind to the wisdom of Christ. Therefore, we should never be swayed by their opinions.
Read 2 Corinthians 4:3–4.
What can unbelievers not see? _____

_____

God "darkens their understanding" (Ephesians 4:18). We live in a very dark world, but as a believer, the true light lives in us.
Read 2 Corinthians 4:6.
What does God give believers? _____

_____

Read the last part of Ephesians 4:18. What caused the ignorance of the Gentiles?

_____

Think of the many people who stopped coming to church, stopped serving, and stopped coming to Bible study. Why? What happened?

The Gentiles' hearts were hardened because they heard the message but did not believe. Therefore, their understanding was darkened.

Remember yesterday's lesson on spiritual infancy? Believers have to grow, moving forward in their work on a daily basis. Babies are meant to become adults. Spiritual infants are meant to mature in Christ. Staying a spiritual infant can lead to becoming stagnant or developing a cold heart.

Read Ephesians 4:19.

What did the Gentiles give into? _____

_____

As believers, if we aren't obtaining God's wisdom and becoming mature in the fullness of Christ, our hearts can become cold, and we can also give into sin.

Read Psalm 51:10, Psalm 119:9, Proverbs 4:23,Ezekiel 36:26, and Matthew 24:12.

What can happen to our hearts if we give into sin? _____

_____

What must we do? _____

_____

Read Ephesians 4:20–24.

What are we to put off? _____

What is to be made new? _____

What are we created to be like? _____

Read 2 Corinthians 5:17.

- A caterpillar was never meant to stay a caterpillar.
- An infant was never meant to stay an infant.
- A seed was never meant to stay a seed.
- A sapling was never meant to stay a sapling.
- A spiritual infant was never meant to stay a spiritual infant.
- To become a butterfly, the caterpillar must grow.

- To become an adult, the infant must grow.
- To become a plant, the seed must grow.
- To become a tree, the sapling must grow.
- To become a mature believer, the spiritual infant must grow.

Is there anything in your life hindering you from growing strong in the Lord? ____

_____

_____

Is there anything in your life hindering you from letting the light of Christ within you shine so that others may see?

_____

Day 5

Types of Anger

Ephesians 4:25–27

Read Ephesians 4:25.

*G*od is the essence of truth.

"I am the way and the truth and the life" (John 14:6).

God expects us to speak truth because He is truth.

Read Exodus 20:16, Psalm 15:2, Proverbs 12:17–20, and Zechariah 8:16. In these, we are commanded to speak the truth.

How can dishonesty wreak havoc in a person's life and spiritual walk? _____

_____

_____

How can dishonesty wreak havoc in a church? _____

_____

_____

When someone chooses to speak untruthful words about another, evil has been plotted. It can cause anger, which leads me to Ephesians 4:26–27. Read those verses.

Write why you think Paul says, "In your anger do not sin," instead of saying, "Do not be angry."

_____

_____

There are two types of anger—righteous anger and sinful anger.

There is absolutely nothing wrong with being angry over an unrighteous act. Give an example of righteous anger here.

_____

_____

Read Matthew 21:12–13.

Why was Jesus angry? _____

_____

Read Psalm 7:11.

God is a righteous judge and gets angry at injustice and sinful behavior. Give an example of sinful anger here.

_____

_____

Read Esther 3:5 and Daniel 3:13.

When our anger becomes about revenge or causes rage, it becomes sinful. When our anger is wrapped up in our emotions and we feel like someone did us wrong, it becomes sinful. When our anger turns into bitterness, it becomes sinful.

When we choose to park ourselves at anger and stay, it's become a sin that can consume us.

Anger should not last. That's why Paul warned us in Ephesians 4:26 to not "let the sun go down while you are still angry." If we do, it will "give the devil a foothold" (verse 27).

Read Proverbs 14:29 and James 1:19–20.

How can sinful anger hurt a church? _____

_____

We can sometimes get hurt the worst by fellow Christians. Unfortunately, when we choose to hold onto that hurt, it can lead to sinful anger and bitterness. That can give the devil a foothold to wreak havoc on the peace of a church body, which is always his plan.

Do not let the sun go down on your anger, my friend.

If you have allowed a seed of bitterness to grow, give it to God. Do not allow an invasive weed to cover your life where good things should grow. Allow God to remove it before it spreads further.

Day 1

Hard Work Pays Off

Ephesians 4:28

Read Ephesians 4:28.

This passage says, "Anyone who has been stealing must steal no longer, but must work, doing something useful with their own hands, that they may have something to share with those in need."

Being the good little Christians we are, it would be easy to read this verse in a prideful manner with our heads held high and think, *I would never steal! I work hard for what I have! I always give to those in need!*

Think again my friend. Let's break this verse into three parts, so that our bubble is not burst all at once.

1. "He who has been stealing must steal no longer."

To Christians, this should be preschool. "Thou shalt not steal." Unfortunately, there are believers who blatantly steal in a criminal way. And of course, this is *wrong*! We should never take anything that is not rightfully ours.

We shouldn't even take from the office supply closet or even pad our taxes!

But what about withholding from the Lord? Are we stealing from the Lord when we do not tithe since everything we have is His?

Read Malachi 3:10–12.

What does God do when we tithe? _____

_____

"Whoever can be trusted with very little can also be trusted with much, and whoever is dishonest with very little will also be dishonest with much" (Luke 16:10).

Are you being dishonest with what has been given to you? Can the Lord trust you with more?

"Now it is required that those who have been given a trust must prove faithful" (1 Corinthians 4:2).

"For we brought nothing into the world, and we can take nothing out of it" (1 Timothy 6:7).

Read Matthew 6:21.

Is your treasure found in hoarding what you have all to yourself? Or are you using what you have to glorify God?

2. "But must work, doing something useful with his own hands."

Paul was no stranger to hard work. Not only did he work tirelessly as a servant of Christ, but he also earned funds as a tent maker. Jesus was a carpenter too.

We were not created to be lazy, to expect an easy life, or to be mere dreamers who never follow through with anything we say.

"Diligent hands will rule, but laziness ends in forced labor" (Proverbs 12:24).

"All hard work brings a profit, but mere talk leads only to poverty" (Proverbs 14:23).

Read 1 Timothy 5:8.

What does the Word say about providing for our family? _____

_____

God expects us to work hard in all that we do. And everything we do must always be to bring Him glory.

"Whatever you do, work at it with all your heart, as working for the Lord, not for human masters" (Colossians 3:23).

3. "That he may have something to share with those in need."

Okay, I'm just going to be blunt here. God means much more here than buying a couple of presents for a child at Christmas or donating the cans of food in the back of your pantry that are about to expire to a local food bank.

Sharing with those in need should be a daily part of our lives.

Read Matthew 25:35.

What are we supposed to do? _____

_____

We should be praying for God to show us opportunities to help those in need *every* day. I'm going to be blunt again. *Sometimes* it's easier to give money to help people (e.g., buying school supplies for a child in need, giving money to someone for a much-needed meal, donating to a local soup kitchen, giving clothes to organizations, etc.).

And we should do these things on a regular basis. If you give twenty-five dollars to Samaritan's Purse, you can provide a well with clean water to five hundred villagers in another country. Fourteen dollars can buy a dozen baby chicks that will provide eggs and income for families in other countries as well. That's two coffee drinks for us.

But what about more? You might say, "I don't have enough money to do more than that." Oh, I'm talking about much more than money.

What about that stranger you bought a meal for? What about sitting with them, listening to their story, and sharing the gospel?

What about that single mom in your church? What about bringing her dinner and keeping her kids for a night to give her a break?

What about teaching people a trade such as sewing, baking, or doing yard work so that they can provide extra funds for their families.

What about the children in your neighborhood, your church, or the school that your child attends who never seem to have anyone around? Offer to throw the baseball with them, take them to the park, or attend a school play together.

Too busy? Too inconvenient? Did the person you gave a meal to look like an addict? Did the single mom not seem appreciative? Does the child have behavior issues?

God doesn't call us to question the motives of those in need. He calls us to share with those in need. Pray over the circumstances and leave the rest up to God.

Ask yourself if you struggle with these acts of generosity.

Be honest with the Lord as you seek to know Him better. Pray that the desires of your heart will line up with His.

Day 2

Power of the Tongue

Ephesians 4:29–31

The Word of God has quite a bit to say on the power of the tongue. What comes out of our mouths can destroy our witness for Christ or bring others to Christ.
Read Ephesians 4:29.
What should *not* come out of our mouth? What *should*? _____

_____

_____

Read the following verses:

- Exodus 23:1,
- Leviticus 19:16,
- Psalm 34:13,
- Proverbs 10:18–19,
- Proverbs 11:9,
- Proverbs 11:13,
- Proverbs 16:28,
- Proverbs 17:9,
- Proverbs 18:8,
- Proverbs 18:21,
- Proverbs 20:19,
- Proverbs 26:20, and
- James 4:11.

Friendships are often destroyed because of secrets. Reputations are ruined because of slander. Churches are torn apart by those who stir the pot.

Why do you think people use their mouths this way? _____

_____

Read James 1:26.

What does this type of tongue do to our witness? _____

_____

Read Psalm 141:3.

What can we do? _____

_____

Read Ephesians 4:30.

What does Paul tell us not to do to the Holy Spirit? _____

_____

The moment we became believers, we were sealed in Christ, and the Holy Spirit dwells in us (Ephesians 1:13).

Paul tells us not to "grieve" the Holy Spirit, and we can translate this as "bring sorrow to."

As church members and believers, there are two things we should not do to the Holy Spirit—quench the Spirit and grieve the Spirit.

"Do not quench the spirit" (1 Thessalonians 5:19).

"And do not grieve the Holy Spirit of God" (Ephesians 4:30).

We "bring sorrow to" the Holy Spirit when we do not live in the "fullness of Christ." We grieve the Spirit when our mouths cause our witnesses to be destroyed, when unwholesome words are spoken, when our critical tongues bring other down, and when our words cause strife within a body of believers.

Read Ephesians 4:31.

Paul tells us to get rid of all bitterness, rage, anger, brawling, slander, and malice.

Read 1 Peter 2:1–2.

What are we to crave? _____

_____

_____

The words that come out of our mouths should *always* bring glory to God. If you have a problem with this, pray for God to heal your tongue and heart.

"Above all else, guard your heart, for everything you do flows from it" (Proverbs 4:23).

What's in your heart will usually flow out of your mouth.

Ask God for protection of both your heart and tongue.

Day 3

Be Kind Anyway

Ephesians 4:32

*M*y favorite verse in the Bible is Ephesians 4:32, yet it is also an extremely challenging verse to live by at all times.

"Be kind and compassionate to one another, forgiving each other just as in Christ God forgave you" (Ephesians 4:32).

When my children were very young, I started a kindness and compassion chart. It was a reward chart of sorts, but we did it in a different manner than all my other reward charts for chores, good behavior, and accomplishments. And we gave rewards in a much different manner as well. As a young parent, it was difficult to live this verse out, and I was often overwhelmed by the lack of kindness I was seeing in children and adults. I wanted to instill in my kids at an early age what really being kind meant.

My kids get a sticker on the chart when they have completed an act of kindness or shown compassion. (We still do this even though they are now fifteen and ten.) The deal is that they can't tell me to put a sticker on their charts for such an act. I have to hear about or see it myself. I want this behavior to become a daily part of their lives. I want kindness and compassion to be like breathing to them. Why? Because God instructs it and our world lacks it. When you show kindness and compassion, you show someone Jesus.

So it takes a long time to fill up one of these charts, but when they do, we have a family celebration. We have the dinner of their choice, and we discuss how we can continue to live out this verse.

The following are examples of kindness and compassionate acts they have gotten stickers for:

- A teacher told me they were the only ones who stood up for a student who was being bullied.
- A teacher told me they were peacemakers between arguing friends.
- Another parent told me they've often encouraged their children.
- They raked an elderly neighbor's yard without anyone asking them.
- They used their own money to buy supplies for Operation Christmas Child.
- They used their own money to buy school supplies for other kids (e.g., uniforms, supplies, backpacks, etc.).
- They befriended the kid no one else would.

I'm so proud of my kids. But through my blinded parental pride, I'm reminded—and I remind them—that this should just simply be part of who we are because the Holy Spirit lives within us.

Now I'm about to address the difficult side of this verse. The acts of kindness and compassion listed previously should be easy for a Christian. The difficult part of the verse is the second part, which is "forgiving each other, just as in Christ God forgave you."

The true test of this verse is being kind and compassionate to those who aren't kind and compassionate to you *and* forgiving them all the while. We live in a world that is all about revenge.

- If someone hurts you, hurt them back!
- If they aren't a good friend, cut them off!
- They don't speak to me, so I'm not speaking to them!
- That person doesn't deserve kindness!

My kids have learned from an early age that my answer is always, "You have to be kind to them anyway. Forgive them. Their meanness probably comes from hurt. Pray for them."

Don't get me wrong. The very human, mama-bear side of me usually begins the conversation by saying, "That was so mean! Why do people act like that?"

But we have to take a deep breath and get biblical!

Read Proverbs 3:3, Luke 6:35, Galatians 5:22–23, and Colossians 3:12.

What do these verses say about kindness? _____

_____

Read Matthew 6:14, Mark 11:25, Luke 17:3–4, and Colossians 3:13.

What do these verses say about forgiving? _____

_____

I have no doubt this is one of the most challenging verses to live by. Mother Teresa of Calcutta said,

> People are often unreasonable and self-centered. Forgive them anyway. If you are kind, people may accuse you of ulterior motives. Be kind anyway. If you are honest, people may cheat you. Be honest anyway. If you find happiness, people may be jealous. Be happy anyway. The good you do today may be forgotten tomorrow. Do good. Give the world the best you have, and it may never be enough. Give your best anyway. For you see, in the end, it is between you and God. It was never between you and them anyway.[20]

As Cinderella would say, "Have courage and be kind."

Day 4

What Are You Imitating?

Ephesians 5:1–2

The definition of *imitator* is "someone who copies the behavior or actions of another."[21]

So who or what are we imitating?

George Washington wrote, "Associate yourself with men of good quality if you esteem your own reputation; for 'tis better to be alone than in bad company."

Mark Ambrose said, "In your free time, you will choose who to hang out with. If you were to show me your friends, I could tell you your future."[22]

John Mason said, "The simple but true fact of life is that you become like those with whom you closely associate—for the good and the bad."

Here is my favorite and probably the most profound quotation from thatonerule.com: "If you hang out with chickens, you're going to cluck, and if you hang out with eagles, you're going to fly."[23]

So if the world is full of clucking chickens, how do we soar like eagles?

We can be influenced so easily in this world. The quotes mentioned previously remind me of several scriptures that caution us to choose our friends wisely.

What do the following verses say about friendship?

Proverbs 12:26: _____

_____

Proverbs 13:20: _____

_____

Proverbs 27:17: _____

_____

I love to see my children display a good quality that I know a family member has instilled in them. It brings parents great joy to see their children imitate a good behavior they have learned at home. But oh, how cringe-worthy it is to see or hear them imitate a behavior that is less than admirable. Children are going to imitate what they see on a consistent basis—the good, the bad, and the ugly.

There are so many animals and insects in this world that mimic the appearance or imitate the behavior of a much more dangerous species to either camouflage themselves or deceive prey. The South America leaf fish simply act like their environment. They look like dead leaves floating in the water. But when seeking their prey, that seemingly dead leaf moves with such speed that their prey doesn't even know what happened.

God never intended for us to live lives clucking like all the rest of the chickens in this world, and He certainly doesn't want us to blend into our environment.

"Do not conform to the pattern of this world, but be transformed by the renewing of your mind. Then you will be able to test and approve what God's will is—his good, pleasing, perfect will" (Romans 12:2).

To be the eagle that soars, you can't fall into the pattern of all the clucking chickens.

What does God's Word say about how we will know what His will is? _____

_____

_____

If we do not know His will, we will blend in with everyone else.
Read Ephesians 5:1.
Who, my friend, are we called to imitate? _____

We are called to live lives that imitate God. Imitators of God do not blend in. Their lives are different, set apart, light in a dark world.
Read Ephesians 5:2.
I think we all like to think we live lives that love *big*.
How can we love those who seem unlovable, who hurt us over and over, and who never seem to be sorry or even care? _____

_____

Read Matthew 22:37–39.

What are the two greatest commandments? _____

_____

_____

Agape love is the most supernatural, selfless form of love that transcends any feeling or emotion that we could ever muster. It is the sacrificial love that Christ showed us on the cross.

To love like Christ is something that we have to pray for daily. If you struggle with loving others, you should pray! The struggle of loving others and living a life of love mentioned in Ephesians 5:2 is very real.

Maybe you struggle with loving family members who have caused hurt over and over again. I pray that you will show them mercy and love them anyway.

Maybe you struggle with loving friends who have rejected you and caused you pain. I pray that you will love them anyway.

Maybe you struggle to love fellow church family members who often criticize you. I pray that you will love them anyway.

Or maybe your struggle with loving others goes much deeper with hurt that is beyond comprehension. I pray that God will heal your heart. I pray that bitterness will be replaced with an inexplicable love. This doesn't mean that a relationship has to continue. It just means God wants to set you free.

To be imitators of Christ and live lives of love is not an easy call. Paul knew he had to remind his friends in Ephesus of this trial because it was something that required commitment, dedication, and prayer.

Don't be a clucking chicken like everyone else. Soar like the eagle God called you to be.

Day 5

Heed Warning

Ephesians 5:3–7

In the opening of Ephesians 5, Paul reminds us to live a life as "imitators of God" and "live a life of love," and this advice serves us well. Paul warns against sinful living. He doesn't sugarcoat anything. They are strong sins that can destroy lives and are very prevalent today. These warnings were on Paul's heart even then.

Read Ephesians 5:3.

This one verse strongly warns against sexual immorality. The KJV and the NIV use the following three warnings:

KJV	NIV
1. Fornication—sexual impurity before marriage. We get the English word *pornography* from the Greek word *fornication*.	1. Sexual immorality.
2. Uncleanness—"morally or spiritually impure." *Merriam-Webster's.*	2. Impurity.
3. Covetousness—"having a craving for" *Merriam-Webster's.*	3. Greed

In Paul's day, sexual immorality was rampant. He knew living a lifestyle of this nature was dangerous and wrong.

Fast-forward to the present day. There are affairs, addictions to pornography, sex trafficking, and much more.

Let's get a little more honest. What about elicit romance novels or extremely popular movies for a girls' night out that are filled with sexual immorality? Do not fool yourselves into thinking that this behavior is okay because it is socially acceptable.

Pray if you struggle with allowing any of these into your life (e.g, pornography, adulterous relationships, movies with socially acceptable sexually behavior, etc.).

Read Ephesians 5:4.

This one verse strongly warns against impurity in our talk.

What three types of talk should we avoid? _____

_____

_____

Do you struggle with this type of talk?

Do you struggle with listening to this type of talk?

At the end of verse 4, Paul tells us what our mouths should do. In the NIV, the passage says, "But rather thanksgiving." In the KJV, it says, "But rather giving of thanks."

Not too long ago, my family was working very hard to save money. I was elated when I received a check for some unclaimed money. I knew nothing about the funds.

That excitement led to disappointment. A week later our perfectly good hot water heater was struck by lightning, and the heating element blew out. We had to replace the whole thing, and I was so disappointed that we had to use our newly saved money almost to the penny.

After my pity party, God made it clear that He had provided. My disappointment quickly turned to gratefulness. Being grateful changes our attitudes immediately.

There is always something to be thankful for. Consider keeping a gratitude journal so that you can document and declare gratefulness and thanksgiving every day.

John Phillips said, "Since we have to talk about something, let us elevate our conversation to a higher plane. Let us use our tongues to express gratitude to God for all that He has done for us and use our conversational skills to encourage others to think seriously about spiritual things."[24]

Does your mouth lead others to Christ or lead them astray? _____

_____

Read Ephesians 5:5–7.

What do immoral people not have? _____

_____

_____

What should we not be deceived by? _____

_____

_____

Be careful who you listen to. Always find the truth in the Word.

In verse 7, what warning is given? _____

_____

_____

Today I want to close with a children's Bible song that is simple yet so profound. Please check out the rest of this profoundly insightful song by searching the web.

"O Be Careful, Little Eyes"

O, be careful little eyes what you see.
O, be careful little eyes what you see.
There's a Father up above,
And He's looking down in love.
So be careful little eyes what you see.[25]

Once we see it, it's in our minds. Once we hear it, we remember it. Once we've done something, the guilt and the consequences follow. Once we have allowed ourselves to go there, it's hard to leave. Once our mouths speak, we cannot take back the words that we have spoken.

So be careful about what you see, what you hear, what you do, where you go, and what you say.

Day 1

Children of Light

Ephesians 5:8–14

Read Ephesians 5:8, which says, "For you were once darkness, but now you are light in the Lord. Live as children of light."

Light is the source that makes things visible. Darkness is the absence of light. As children of light, we can no longer exist in the darkness of sin. Living an immoral life that Paul referred to in the previous verses of chapter 5 (vv. 3–7) would not shine forth the illumination of Christ.

The flame from a candle will not produce a shadow of any kind. Go ahead and try it! Hold a candle or a flame against a wall, and you will see only the shadows of the candle itself, not a shadow of the flame. There is no darkness in light. God is so amazing that His truth is evident even in a physical flame.

"The light shines in the darkness, and the darkness has not overcome it" (John 1:5).

Living as children of light produces fruit.

Read Ephesians 5:9.

What fruits of light are mentioned in this verse? _____

_____

_____

God is good. God is righteous. God is truth.

Children of light will display these qualities because we are "imitators of God" (Ephesians 5:1).

Read Romans 12:9. What does this verse say about goodness? _____

_____

Read Psalm 112:6. What does this verse say about being righteous? _____

_____

Read 1 John 3:18. What does this verse say about truth? _____

_____

Are you living a life that displays the fruit of light? If so, how? If not, why not? _____

_____

_____

Read Ephesians 5:10.
What does Paul encourage us to do in this verse? _____

_____

_____

How do we find out what is pleasing to the Lord or acceptable to Him?

A good start is lining our lives up with how Jesus lived. Judging our actions (or lack of action) based on how Jesus Christ Himself lived.

In the 1990s, a popular motto with the abbreviation WWJD surfaced. This acronym stands for the question "What would Jesus do?" It was primarily put on bracelets and worn as a reminder to question your own decisions and actions. We, too, could look at Paul's advice in verse 10 and question ourselves before we make any decision.

Is this acceptable to the Lord?

Is this pleasing to Him?

If we find that the action or answer doesn't line up with God's character, which is good, righteous, and true, then we shouldn't move forward. Our answer is no. Remember, there is no darkness in light. God is light, and in Him, there is no darkness. There aren't ever gray areas, my friend.

Do you find yourself trying to justify behaviors, decisions, actions that seem gray? Do you tell yourself that these acts aren't that bad? _____

_____

_____

Read Ephesians 5:11–14.

What are we to do with fruitless deeds of darkness? _____

_____

What is exposed in the light? _____

_____

You cannot live a secret life of sin and also live as a child of light. Eventually, the light exposes everything.

Is there any part of your life that is filled with secret sin? _____

_____

_____

Ask God to wake you from your slumber and to be more aware of how the darkness is affecting your spiritual walk.

Day 2

Seize the Day
Ephesians 5:15–17

Read Ephesians 5:15–17.

Now that I'm older, I've often found myself saying to my husband, "What did we do with all our time back in the day?" We were married for five years before we had our first child. He pastored a church while he was working on his doctorate. I was a fourth-grade schoolteacher at the time. Yes, that kept us busy. But then I look at our lives now! We have two kids and various ministries. He is a senior pastor, and I have part-time jobs. There's volunteer work and coaching too. We must have had an enormous amount of free time before all that. If I could go back to those five years—and they were good, sweet years—I would definitely use my time more wisely. I would be more kingdom-focused early on. Oh, I thought I was, but I wasted a lot of time.

For today's homework, I want you to get a calendar, journal, or just some paper. I want you to keep a log of what you do every hour for one week. Where is most of your time spent? Where do you have downtime or free time? Be honest with yourself. If you watch two hours of TV a day, log that time. If you spent ten to fifteen minutes every hour on the hour on social media, log that too. At the end of each day, categorize your day—work for eight hours, housework for one hour, grocery shopping for one hour, dinner for one hour, TV for two hours, social media for two hours, prayer for one hour, Bible study for one hour, and so on.

Remember to be completely honest. God already knows how you spend your time, and you don't have to show this to anyone else.

Look and see how much time you spend on the kingdom.

How much time did you spend leading others to Christ? _____

How much time did you spend in prayer? _____

How much time did you spend studying the Word? _____

    If this way of keeping track of your time was helpful in recognizing time that is spent wisely or unwisely, then you can continue the practice!

    Pray for God to help you make the most of every opportunity.

Day 3

Filled with the Spirit

Ephesians 5:18–21

Read Ephesians 5:18.

There is no question that the wine of today is different from the wine in biblical days. Paul is clear in verse 18 on what *not* to do. The topic of alcohol has been debated and debated and debated. The consumption of alcohol, drunkenness, and alcoholism has destroyed families, marriages, and lives.

Should a Christian drink? Pray, my friend, over this choice, and let God guide you. Also ask yourself, "Is this hurting my testimony? Is this leading others to Christ?" (You could also ask these question about any choice we make.)

Paul tells us what *not* to do in verse 18, but he also tells us what we should do instead. What is it? _____

_____

_____

Can someone be a Christian and not be filled with the Spirit? _____

_____

The Holy Spirit dwells within every Christian who has been born again. But there is spiritual infancy, and then there are those Christians who are mature in Christ. We have covered both these in this study.

What do you think being filled with the Spirit means? _____

_____

Imagine being in a dessert and walking for miles. You long for water. It's hot and humid. It's been hours since you had any. You finally reach your destination. You are handed a cup of water, but there are only a few drops in it. It certainly doesn't quench your thirst. Who wants an almost empty cup of water?

Okay, maybe this is a more accurate scenario: You went to bed late. You are tired and cranky. It's Monday too! Your hope for sanity comes in the form of coffee. You tirelessly reach the kitchen, fill the pot with water, reach for your coffee supply, and you are out! An empty bag of coffee makes for a rough Monday.

Have you attended tons of Bible studies and church services and wonder why you still feel spiritually empty? Does something still not feel satisfying even though you are a believer? It's like your car. You have to fill it up with gas, right? And it's not a one-time thing.

When our lives are not full of the Spirit, our spiritual tank is on empty. Our salvation is still sealed, but our walk is empty. This is a big factor in doubting your salvation as well.

If you know that your salvation is sealed but you doubt it over and over again, what is lacking? _____

_____

Do you really need to pray the prayer *again*? Maybe you just need to fill your Holy Spirit tank.

Remember all the sins Paul warned us about in the beginning of chapter 5?
Read Galatians 5:16–18.
What is in conflict with each other? _____

_____

We cannot be full of the Spirit and full of sin.
Read Galatians 5:22–24. Write verse 24 here. _____

_____

_____

To live a life full of the Spirit is to have such fruit displayed in our lives.
Read Ephesians 5:19–20.
What kind of fruit of the Spirit does this bring to mind? _____
Joy, sister! It brings supernatural joy!
Read Galatians 5:25.

How can we keep in step with the Spirit? _____

_____

Being full of the Spirit requires submission to the Spirit daily. We slack off. We become empty.

"Fill my cup, Lord; I lift it up, Lord. Come and quench this thirsting of my soul. Bread of Heaven, feed me till I want no more. Fill my cup, fill it up and make me whole."[26]

Let's close today with Ephesians 5:21, which says, "Submit to one another out of reverence for Christ."

Paul leads us perfectly into relationships that we will cover in the rest of chapter 5 and the beginning of chapter 6.

Day 4

Wives

Ephesians 5:22–24

Please read Ephesians 5:22–24.

Paul made it clear in verse 22 that wives are to submit to their husbands as they *first* submit to the Lord.

Read 1 Corinthians 11:3.

Write the three headships mentioned in this verse. _____

_____

_____

Paul is addressing believers in Ephesians 5:22–24. True submission is done out of love and respect. This sort of biblical marriage does not equate a superior and an inferior. It is a mutual relationship—one done in Christ and through love. As Paul tells wives to submit to their husbands, he is assuming the husbands are believers. But what if your husband isn't a believer?

Read 1 Peter 3:1–6.

What words of wisdom does Peter give to wives whose husbands do not believe? _____

_____

_____

Where does Peter say beauty should come from? _____

_____

In 1 Peter 3:6, what does Peter warn against? _____

_____

There are so many wives whose husbands are not living in full submission to the Lord. They are trying to be godly wives, godly mothers, and godly friends. Yet their heart aches for their household to be in the biblical hierarchy mentioned in 1 Corinthians 11:3.

What is a wife to do?

Ephesians 5:24 says, "Now as the church submits to Christ, so also wives should submit to their husbands in everything."

Everything!

Remember, this passage of scripture is written for believers. Nowhere in the Bible does it say to submit or follow your husband into sin. Please seek Christian counseling if you find yourself in this situation.

Pray over your marriage. Pray for your husband every single day.

And as you lift up those prayers, pray that God will guide and direct you as the wife you should be. We are bombarded with movies, TV, magazines, and other people who surround us. The world does not uphold this sort of biblical union.

Read Proverbs 31:10–31.

From the previous passage, list the characteristics a godly wife should possess. _____

_____

_____

The world puts so much pressure on women today. We are supposed to be like Superwoman, right?

I really never wanted to be Superwoman. I always wanted to be Wonder Woman with the lasso of truth and the invisible jet.

But I'm usually a different type of Wonder Woman. I wonder where my keys are *all the time*. I wonder how I'm going to get everything done. I wonder if I'm doing a good job at everything. Am I a good mother? A good wife?

There is actually a handbook for this thing called life. It's called the Bible. Let's quit pressuring ourselves to be anything but what God called us to be.

Pray over the virtues a Proverbs 31 woman lives by. Use them as a guide in your life so that you can be a godly woman.

Day 5

Husbands

Ephesians 5:25–33

*I*n yesterday's lesson we studied Ephesians 5:22–24. Paul stressed that wives are to submit to their husbands just as the church submits to Christ. Today we see Paul linking the love that Christ has for the church to the love a husband should have for his wife.

Read Ephesians 5:25–33.

We live in a world where we set constant expectations. We live in a world where we set the bar at give-and-take.

- I pay the electric bill. I expect electricity.
- I pay at a restaurant. I expect the food I ordered.
- I put gas in my car. I expect it to go.

And at home, my husband and I have learned various give-and-take routines that work well.

- I cook. Jay puts the leftovers in the fridge.
- I load the dishwasher. Jay unloads the dishwasher.

I'm sure you get my point. What happens when my electricity goes out for a few hours (just in the middle of cooking) because of a storm? Do I not pay my bill?

What if I cook a lavish meal and Jay forgets to put the leftovers up before bed? Do I put them up or let them spoil?

These are rhetorical questions, of course.

Wives are to submit. Husbands are to take care of and love their wives.

What if you get mad at your husband because he isn't meeting your needs? Do you quit submitting?

And as a wife, if you override the submission, is a husband supposed to stop taking care of or loving his wife?

Do you expect more than your husband can give?

Paul was wise enough to know that a godly marriage of believers is still needed. This is sound advice because marriage is hard.

We may give and give and may not always be given anything in return. There will be seasons that are harder than others, but we must continue to give our spouses what God calls us to give.

You may be dating or newly married. You may feel an eight-year itch, or you may have reached the fifty-year milestone. You may be broken and divorced, healed and divorced, approaching divorce, or never married at all.

Whatever personal season you are in, go to battle in prayer. Pray for your own situation or for those closest to you.

Go to battle in prayer for your future marriage or the marriage of your children.

Go to battle for protection of the good marriage you are in.

Go to battle for the marriage you are in that is falling apart.

Go to battle for the marriages within your church.

Read 1 Peter 3:7 and write it here. _____

_____

_____

Pray for your man, the men in your family, and the men in your church so that they will rise up and be the husbands God called them to be.

I've been married for twenty years as I write this, *two decades plus dating*. There has been lots of romance, lots of love, lots of aggravation, lots of raising kids, lots of life and business.

We must never mistake the absence of romance for the absence of love. But we cannot stay there either!

When was the last time you pursued your husband? When did you last write him a love letter? Flirted with him? Are those days long gone for you? They shouldn't be. Are you waiting for him to make the first move? *He doesn't do it anymore, so why should I?* you may think.

Come on, ladies. We aren't two-year-olds who throw temper tantrums, or are we? I'm not sure that look will look good on us.

Read Song of Songs. Pray for God to put the spark back in your marriage. Do you want compliments? So does your husband.

Week 7

Day 1

Respect Authority

Ephesians 6:1–9

As parents, we have a biblical responsibility to teach our children to respect authority. One of the first lessons in life for children is learning to obey and respect their parents. Later in a child's life, this lesson will roll over into respecting teachers, professors, law enforcement, and bosses in the workplace.

Read Ephesians 6:1–3.

Read Exodus 20:12.

Ephesians 6:2 quotes Exodus 20:12, which says, "Honor your father and mother." This is the fifth commandment of the Ten Commandments.

Paul mentioned a promise in Ephesians 6:2–3. What is promised if this commandment is lived out?

_____

_____

I've always thought there would be so much time to teach my children everything I possibly could about how important their walk with the Lord is. I cannot count how many children's Bible studies, devotion books, and journals I've bought them. Some were very well used, and some were never opened. I post scripture in their rooms and the bathroom, and I pack the Word in their lunch boxes. But baseball games, tennis matches, soccer tournaments, dance classes, good times spent with friends, and more have also filled our days. There have been chaotic nights filled with too much homework and too little sleep.

It's not easy fitting God into our schedule sometimes. I will never be a perfect parent, but if I spend too many days thinking that I've got to fit God into our schedule, then something is way off balance.

Refocus, regroup, and renew.

We have to teach our children that God is first and everything else is second. If our lives get too hectic, slow down, pray for focus, and get things back in order.

"Be still and know that I am God" (Psalm 46:10).

As a parent, we must teach our children that their walk with the Lord cannot be something that we just try to fit into our schedule.

Read Deuteronomy 6:4–9.

When should we teach our children about the Lord? _____

_____

_____

Read Proverbs 22:6 and write it here. _____

_____

_____

If we teach our children to respect authority as a commandment for the Lord, and if we train them up in the way they should go, we will lay a foundation in their lives that is priceless because it's biblical. Parenting is the hardest and the most joyful gift. God has given us this wisdom in scripture to train them up. We cannot ignore this first step in the training. If you leave out the flour in a baking recipe, there will be no substance. Do not leave out teaching your children to honor, love, and respect you. There will be no foundation for them if you don't. And if we want our children to respect us, we have to teach all of this in love.

Read Ephesians 6:5–9.

In these verses we see where Paul transitions respect and obeying authority to the workplace. Thank God that slavery has been abolished, but that doesn't mean we skip over these verses and ignore them. If you work, you answer to authority.

Read Ephesians 6:6–7 again.

What should our motives be when we're working, volunteering, or serving? _____

_____

_____

So maybe you are the boss in the workplace or the chair of a committee in church or a volunteer in an organization. Never misuse your place of authority and belittle others.

Read Ephesians 6:9 again.

Paul made the importance of honoring, respecting, and loving those around us very clear. From the time we are tots to parentals to employees or bosses, R-E-S-P-E-C-T. You've got to find out what it means to you. Apparently, it means a lot to the Lord.

Day 2

The Armor of God

Ephesians 6:10–13

Read Ephesians 6:10–13.

Remember that Paul is writing this while chained up as a prisoner in a Roman jail. He knows the battle we are fighting on this earth is real and that our enemy wants to destroy us from the moment we first become Christians.

For some background info on the fall of Satan, read Isaiah 14 and Ezekiel 28.

Satan seeks to distract you with busyness, depression, and turmoil. He wants to destroy our families, tear apart our churches, and just wreak havoc in our lives.

What does Paul tell us to put on in Ephesians 6:11? _____

_____

Why? _____

_____

_____

According to Ephesians 6:12, who is our struggle and battle against? _____

_____

_____

Our struggles on this earth may *seem* to be with people, but our struggles are not against flesh and blood.

There is a battle raging all around us that we cannot visually see against the angels and demons in the heavenly realms. Sounds scary, right? Well, it is. You would never go to war without weapons and protection, right? This is exactly the point Paul is trying to make us aware of.

Real 1 Peter 5:8–11.

What is Peter's warning? _____

_____

The greatest news is that God already won the war against Satan. Jesus Christ is our victory over death and sin. Boom! Take that Satan!

But the battle is raging here on earth, and we have to be prepared. We can't do it alone, unprotected, or unprepared. Do not ignore this because it scares you. God not only fights the battle with us and for us but also provides spiritual armor for protection so that we can fight the enemy.

Read 1 Samuel 17:47.

Whose battle is it? _____

Read 2 Chronicles 20:15.

Whose battle is it? _____

Know that whatever you are facing, the battle is not yours to fight alone. Are you armed? Are you prepared? Be ready for the battle, my friend.

Day 3

Pieces of Armor

Ephesians 6:14–17

" *S* tand against the devil's schemes" (Ephesians 6:11).
"You may be able to *stand* your ground" (Ephesians 6:13).
"*Stand* firm then" (Ephesians 6:14).

If you play or watch sports of any kind, you know that if people are knocked to the ground, their opponents have an advantage for victory. In the game of life, Paul knew that our opponent in battle wants us knocked down. Paul gives us a warning to *stand*, be alert, be prepared, and be ready.

There are six pieces of spiritual armor that we have to intentionally put on daily. Without them, we head into battle unprotected and unprepared. Would a football player ever play a game without a helmet, a mouth guard, pads, cleats, or a football? Would a scuba diver ever dive without the proper suit and breathing tank? Would a fireman ever attempt to fight a fire without protective clothing, a smoke mask, and a hose? Sounds foolish, right? Why would we ever start our days without being protected and armed for battle?

Read Ephesians 6:14–17.

1. The Belt of Truth—Ephesians 6:14

A Roman soldier would first put on a leather belt that had protective brass plates hanging in front for protection. The belt also provided the means for a soldier to tuck in excess fabric from the typically worn tunic in case he needed to run or move quickly. This is what the phrase "Gird your loins" means in the Bible.

Read Jeremiah 1:17.

The belt of truth is the first piece of spiritual armor to prepare you for battle. You must be prepared with the truth of Jesus Christ.

Does your life demonstrate integrity, honesty, and trustworthiness? _____

_____

Read the following verses and make notes on what you believe the Word says about integrity, honesty, and trustworthiness.

1 Chronicles 29:17: _____

_____

Proverbs 10:9: _____

_____

Proverbs 12:22: _____

_____

Ephesians 4:25: _____

_____

Colossians 3:9: _____

_____

2 Timothy 2:15: _____

_____

1 John 3:18: _____

_____

We must be armed with the truth of scripture and be witnesses of integrity whom people can trust.

2. The Breastplate of Righteousness—Ephesians 6:14

A Roman soldier's second piece of armor would have been a metal or chain breastplate. This piece would protect the soldier's vital organs, primarily his heart and lungs. Without a beating heart and breath in his lungs, a soldier would surely die.

The Spirit of the one who gives us breath in our lungs and pumps our heart lives within us.

Read 2 Corinthians 5:21.

What might we become because of Christ? _____

_____

_____

Can we earn righteousness by good deeds? _____

Read Titus 3:5, Galatians 2:20–21, and Philippians 3:9.

Righteousness cannot be earned. It is a gift that has been imputed to us.

So how do we live a life of righteousness?

My doctrinally sound theological answer?

Do the right thing. Always.

Do what is right in the Lord and what will bring Him glory. And we can only live this way through the saving power of Jesus Christ, who dwells within us. Through His strength we can live a life of righteousness.

"Above all else, guard your heart, for everything you do flows from it" (Proverbs 4:23).

3. The Gospel of Peace—Ephesians 6:15

As the third piece of armor for a Roman soldier, his shoes were studded with hobnails to provide a firm foundation for standing without slipping.

In my mind, putting on shoes means we are about to go somewhere. As Christians, we should always be ready to go—go spread the Word, go be witnesses for the Lord, go serve.

"Go into all the world and preach the gospel to all creation" (Mark 16:15).

When a Roman soldier put on his shoes for battle, he was ready to go. But he also didn't have to worry about stepping on debris that could slow him down or cause pain.

The lack of worry is the production of peace.

Do you have supernatural peace in your life? When trials come your way, do the hobnails on your armored shoes lessen the blow? Or do you feel barefoot and shocked by the pain from the debris all around you?

Read Philippians 4:6–7 and write it here. _____

_____

_____

The "peace that passes all understanding" is what we need, and this type of peace cannot be explained (Philippians 4:7).

God also calls us to be united in peace. Within a church body, how can a church effectively serve if her members are not at peace with one another?

Read 1 Thessalonians 5:13 and John 13:35.

How are we to live with one another? _____

_____

_____

Are your shoes on tightly? Are you standing strong with a foundation of peace within your life and ready to go united in peace with other believers?

4. The Shield of Faith—Ephesians 6:16

What can you extinguish from the evil one with your shield of faith? _____

_____

A Roman soldier never went to battle without his shield. His huge shield was at least four feet tall and three feet wide. This type of shield provided protection for almost his entire body. Soldiers would even put their shields together to form an indestructible testudo formation (aka tortoise shell).

The enemy knows our weaknesses. He throws fiery darts of temptation that he designs to penetrate our weak spots. Our shield of faith provides protection for our whole self.

"And lead us not into temptation, but deliver us from the evil one" (Matthew 6:13).

Your faith should be bigger than the temptation to sin. Is it?

Read 1 Corinthians 10:13.

Remember the tortoise shell formation the Roman soldiers used? There is strength in numbers, my friend. A church family is so important. Christian fellowship and friendship is vital.

Read Ecclesiastes 4:9–12.

How can we help each other as believers? _____

_____

_____

Hold up your shield of faith, my sister, so that the Lord can extinguish the evil arrows thrown your way.

Write Psalm 28:7 here. _____

_____

_____

5. The Helmet of Salvation—Ephesians 6:17

A Roman soldier never went to battle without his helmet to protect his skull. Trauma to the head would have been the end for a soldier.

Our battle begins at the moment of salvation.

Read the following verses about salvation: Romans 10:9–10, Ephesians 1:13–14, and Hebrews 7:25.

It's no coincidence that the piece of armor that signifies our salvation in the Lord is also the piece that guarded a soldier's head. The enemy viciously targets a believer's thoughts.

One of my strongest temptations is my mind. Satan wreaks havoc in my thoughts when I do not intentionally protect my mind with this piece of armor. I believe this is true of many women.

Our thoughts can run rampant when the enemy fires his flaming arrows at our minds—depression, insecurities, unworthiness, hopelessness, despair, lies, torment, anxiety, feelings of rejection. The enemy knows the spots. And when these arrows hit, distraction sets in.

Read Romans 12:2.

How can we know God's will? _____

_____

Read Proverbs 3:5, 2 Corinthians 10:5, Philippians 4:8, and Colossians 3:2. How can God's truths in these scriptures help us guard our minds?

_____

_____

God loves you and me so much! He doesn't want Satan's lies to consume our minds! Read Romans 8:38–39.

What should this verse mean to you? _____

_____

6. The Sword of the Spirit—Ephesians 6:17

Every Roman soldier needed a weapon to defend himself. A soldier would never go into battle without his sword.

What does Ephesians 6:17b say our sword is? _____

Our greatest defense against our enemy is the Word of God.

This one will be short and sweet because it's plain and simple. As a believer, you *have* to know His Word. You can't use it as a weapon if you don't know it and hide it in your heart (Psalm 119:11).

Write Hebrews 4:12 here. _____

_____

_____

Boom! Enough said.

Before your feet hit the floor each day, put your spiritual armor on and be prepared for the battle you are in.

Day 4

Go to Battle in Prayer

Ephesians 6:18–20

Once you are ready for battle with your spiritual armor in place, go to battle in prayer.

Read Ephesians 6:18–19.

If you saw the movie *War Room*, I'm sure you were inspired to construct your own war room. In the movie Miss Clara has a closet that she calls her "war room." Filled with scripture and prayer requests, she meets the Lord in battle every day. She meets Him in prayer intentionally.

God spoke to me through that portion of the movie. I really felt convicted to look at my own prayer life.

Did I pray daily? Yes.

The Lord and I have a constant dialogue throughout the day. And yes, I pray every single day. But do I go to battle in prayer?

I sat down one day and asked God to guide me in prayer for myself because up to that point, I'm ashamed to say, I think most of my prayer life for my family had been for the most part superficial. "Bless my husband. Help him to be a good pastor." "Bless my children. Help them to do well in school today."

Okay, they were deeper than that sometimes. But I had never prayed for them that I felt like I was actually in battle for them. I was specifically led to verses for each of us and guided in prayers that I never knew we needed. I wrote the scripture and the topics of the

prayer out, and I went to battle for more than two hours, weeping and fighting for my family. I've provided a picture of my prayer board.

If you've never experienced this type of prayer, I urge you to pray that God will guide you into it.

Read the following verses on prayer and record your thoughts:

Job 22:27: _____

_____

Psalm 141:2: _____

_____

Psalm 145:18: _____

_____

Jeremiah 29:12: _____

_____

Mark 11:24: _____

_____

Romans 12:12: _____

_____

Colossians 4:2: _____

_____

1 Thessalonians 5:17: _____

_____

James 5:13: _____

_____

1 John 5:14: _____

_____

In Ephesians 6:18, when and what does Paul say to pray about? _____

_____

What warning does he give? _____

_____

What does Paul ask for in Ephesians 6:19–20? _____

_____

The sin of pride sometimes prevents me from asking for anything for myself in prayer. I love that Paul asked for prayer for himself. He knew he needed it. We all do when we're doing the will of the Father.

What does your prayer life really look like? _____

_____

_____

Day 5

Final Greetings

Ephesians 6:21–24

Read Ephesians 6:21–24.

Tychicus was a fellow minister. He helped keep information about Paul up to date with the church of Ephesus. You can imagine how concerned they must have been over the well-being of Paul. And with Paul's closing of his letter, that's a wrap for us.

I am overcome with emotions as I write this day.

The amount of time I have spent with the Lord and in His Word writing this study has been precious. I opened this study with the disclaimer that I'm not a Bible scholar, and I close with the same statement.

What I do know is that the Lord spoke to me clearer than I've ever heard Him before throughout the process of this study.

My prayer is that not only will you be inspired to open the Word and study with Him but that you will also intentionally follow through with a conviction.

What spoke to you the most from this study? _____

_____

_____

Where do you go from here to study His Word? _____

_____

Let's close with Jeremiah 9:23–24.

I pray that you will know and understand God better each day.

Endnotes

1   Photo used by permission of Leon Mauldin (www. bleon1.wordpress.com/2010/page/12/)

2   *Merriam-Webster's.*

3   *Merriam-Webster's.*

4   *Merriam-Webster's.*

5   *Merriam-Webster's.*

6   Wooden roller coaster (July 3, 2017).. In *Wikipedia, The Free Encyclopedia*. Retrieved on July 15, 2017, from https://en.wikipedia.org/w/index.php?title=Wooden_roller_coaster&oldid=788721206.

7   Moody, Macarthur.

8   Macmillan.

9   *Merriam-Webster's.*

10 Dictionary.com.

11 Cornerstone (April 16, 2017). In *Wikipedia, The Free Encyclopedia*. Retrieved on July 31, 2017, from https://en.wikipedia.org/w/index.php?title=Cornerstone&oldid=775643190.

12 Moody, MacArthur.

13 Chosen Books.

14 *Cambridge Dictionary.*

15 Macmillan.

16 *Oxford Dictionary.*

17 Taken from *Exploring Ephesians & Philippians: An Expository Commentary*, copyright 1993 by John Phillips. Published by Kregel Publications, Grand Rapids, MI. Used by permission of the publisher. All rights reserved.

18 Dictionary.com.

19 *Oxford Dictionary.*

20 Hiding Place—Chosen Books.

21 *Oxford Dictionary.*

22 Great-quotes.com/quotes/author/Mark/Ambrose.

23 Thatonerule.com.

24 Phillips commentary, p 142.

25 childbiblesongs.com.

26 hymnal.net/en/hymn/ns/340

Printed in the United States
By Bookmasters